'Love Loyalty'

The Close and Perilous Siege of Basing House
During the English Civil War, 1643–45

Wilfrid Emberton

Copyright © Sharon Allmark, nee Emberton, 1972, 2022.

First published by W.J. Emberton, 1972.

Sharon Allmark, nee Emberton has asserted her right to be identified as the author of this work.

All rights reserved.

No part of this publication may be reproduced, stored in any retrieval system, or transmitted, in any form, or by any means, electronic, mechanical, photocopying, recording, or otherwise, without the prior written permission of the publishers.

To Susan

Whose love, loyalty and understanding means more than I can express or she can imagine.

FOREWORD BY BRIGADIER PETER YOUNG
D.S.O., M.C., M.A., F.S.A., F.R.Hist.S.

The British Isles are studded with the ruins that "Cromwell knocked about a bit" and although Oliver gets a certain amount of discredit for Thomas Cromwell's misdeeds, Basing House was one of those Royalist fortresses that received his personal attention. He stormed the place on October 14th 1645 and after his soldiers had put a number of the small garrison to the sword he destroyed not only its fortifications, but the fine 16th century house itself.

But Cromwell's siege was not the only one the place sustained. The garrison repulsed a dangerous assault in November 1643 when Sir William Waller's men lost heavily and withdrew to Farnham, their morale seriously impaired.

For 24 weeks in 1644 the house which had been fortified with earth works whose main bastions may still be seen, held out against an army and was relieved when things were growing desperate by Colonel Sir Henry Gage whose swift surprise march from Oxford was one of the most skillful exploits of the civil war.

In these pages Wilfrid Emberton, himself an inhabitant of Basing, has evoked its past and the days when no Roundhead could ride down the A30 without risking ambush by the brave and wily Cornet Bryan and his fellows. To achieve this he has not only done a great deal of research but has hazarded his person many times in the battle reenactments of the Sealed Knot in order to steep himself in the techniques of 17th century warfare.

Military history it would seem is a popular subject these days. Conflict whether in the battle field, the council chamber, or the court room makes good drama, as anyone with a television set must know. Perhaps people study old wars in the hope that by knowing about them and how they came to pass they may play some part in preventing new ones. However that may be the civil wars are part of the Heritage of the English speaking people. Great issues were at stake. This, the last struggle fought out on English soil is worthy of study at every level. For this reason I am happy to have the opportunity to commend my friends book about that garrison of Londoners, Hampshire men, Roman Catholics and Anglicans, who defended a third rate fortress three hundred years ago and lived up to their Governor's proud motto AIMEZ LOYAUTE.

Peter Young
RIPPLE
January 1972

PREFACE

This is a book that I just had to write. Living so close to Basing House, my desultory researches into the fortifications over some years gradually turned into a burning interest in the deeds performed there by our fighting ancestors.

The documents which I have perused at the Records Office and elsewhere had actually come from their hands and formed a tangible link with their times, proving them to be no cardboard figures from some school book but actual flesh and blood characters with the same weaknesses and strengths as ourselves, whether they were clad in the peacock garments of the Cavalier or the sober attire of the Roundhead. The ancient Egyptians believed that to speak the name of the dead made them live again. Before I had finished compiling some 100,000 words of notes that boiled down into the finished manuscript, Paulet, Peake, Norton, Rawdon and the others became real living persons that came and stood by my elbow as I wrote. My only wish is that I can convey the same vision to my readers. The danger in the close study of any facet of a war is that the war in its entirety tends to get out of focus. There is a liability to get so absorbed in the local scene that one forgets that here is a small part of a very large jigsaw. In this narrative I have tried to avoid this pitfall by showing how national events affected the siege as well as more local happenings. In a work of this nature one is greatly assisted and encouraged by the help, freely and generously given by all kinds of people. The greatest debt I owe is to Brigadier Peter Young, D.S.O., M.C., M.A., F.S.A., whose eminence as a Civil War historian is too well known to need recounting. I am grateful to him not only for writing the foreword, and reading the manuscript, but in particular for founding the Sealed Knot Society of Cavaliers and Roundheads, causing life to take on a new breadth and interest. By experiencing the battle conditions of the 17th century one is brought to a better understanding and a fuller knowledge of those times. The derisive modern term "Get Knotted", has taken on a new meaning for all of us who enjoy the privilege of membership. My thanks are also due to:—

Mr. G. Marmaduke Alington of Swinhope Hall whose kindness and interest helped me to fill in missing pieces in the jig saw and provided the hitherto unpublished protrait of his ancestor Sir Marmaduke Rawdon.

Mr. A.F. Whitaker, M.A. City Archivist of Winchester, Mr. H.G.A. Booth, A.T.D.AMA, curator of the Willmer House Museum, Farnham. Mr. L. Southern, LL.B, Town Clerk of Newbury. Mr. S.H. Horrocks, F.L.A., Borough Librarian, Reading. Mr. A. Ford. F.I.M.T.A., A.A.C.C.A, Town Clerk of Henley, The Deputy Secretary of the Royal Horticultural Society,. Mr. J. Cole of Chalton and lastly the present owner of Basing House ruins the Hon, P.C. Orde-Paulet, M.A., a direct descendant of the 5th Marquess of Winchester, with whom I discussed certain theories of mine concerning the defences and the treasure legend, and who gave me permission to use the portrait of his ancestor.

I am grateful to the authorities and staff of the British Museum, Bodleian Library, Public Records Office, Guildhall Library, and smaller libraries almost beyond number for their unfailing courtesy and help to me in my researches and in some cases their permission to use photos and quotations in my narrative.

Wilfrid Emberton

OLD BASING

1972

PREFACE TO SECOND EDITION

It is twenty one years since the first publication of Wilfrid Emberton's book and nine years since Wilfrid's untimely death in 1984. During those years the site of Basing House has seen some dramatic changes both in appearance and interpretation of its remains, and so it was a pleasure to be asked by Wilfrid's daughter, Mrs. Sharon Allmark, to write a few lines to update this second edition with these changes.

The site is now owned by Hampshire County Council who purchased the ruins and grounds in 1972. Under County Council management a great deal of clearance and consolidation work has been carried out to the fabric but it will require many more years of work to get the ruins back to the condition they were when first excavated at the turn of the century. Archaeological investigation has also continued, concentrating particularly upon the area of the "Old House" gateway. These works revealed a succession of entrances culminating in the great four turreted gatehouse behind which the Marquis made his final stand. The earlier gatehouse was equipped with a drawbridge which pivoted into a three metre deep pit which still survives built into the Tudor bridge abutment. During these excavations it became apparent that the great circular bank which encloses the "Old House" was on the northern circuit, at least, considerably lower in the past than at present. That this was the case during the siege seems to be confirmed by the only two known contemporary views of the House which had long been considered to be inaccurate in this detail. It now seems probable that the "Old House" bank was heightened and the present encircling brick wall which caps it, constructed at the end of the 17th century as part of a massive landscaping of the site by the 6th Marquis of Winchester to complement his new mansion then under construction next to Grange Barn. It was this landscaping work which finally destroyed Basing House. The remains of tall chimneys (local oral tradition still describes a forest of chimneys at Basing) and shattered towers were tumbled into there own cellars and tons of top soil were wheelbarrowed in to cover them. Where William, 1st Marquis of Winchester, dined King Henry VIII in "his poor house", one hundred and sixty years later, grape vines grew to the delight of Charles, 6th Marquis, prominent supporter of William of Orange.

A less pleasant image is conjured up of the last hour of the siege and the slaughter that ensued by the discovery in 1991 of a small blocked gateway leading from the "Old" to the "New" House. A shallow surface water drain was found at the bottom of the fill and laying next to it was an upturned human skull. The skull was of an individual in his mid twenties and had sustained a sword blow across the top of his head which had then been hacked off. There was no other remains found and it would appear that the decapitated head had rolled, or had been kicked into the drain during the last minutes before the house was finally taken.

Other, less gruesome evidence of the siege can still be seen within the Old House in the form of the remains of two hollow rectangular brick towers constructed through the earlier Tudor Kitchens on either side of the great gatehouse. These were probably filled with earth and rubble and used as artillery platforms to cover the approaches to the bridge.

On the eastern flank of the Old House stood the much grander and larger New House which at the time of writing, very few surviving remains are visible, with the exception that is, of the so called "Roman Well" a massive 50ft deep by lift wide brick lined shaft of Tudor date. The Victorian diggers followed foundation lines but as with the "Old House", after 1922 they were allowed to grass over again.

The New House platform, which formed a raised inner courtyard, caused Cromwell's troops trouble and they were forced to bring up scaling ladders. Today it is pock marked by disturbance from unrecorded digs and treasure hunting activities. The eastern face of the platform has considerable brick remains of what was presumably the inner face of basements belonging to a central wing, the outer face was destroyed by the Basingstoke Canal which in the 1790's cut the New House in half. The outer courtyard and surrounding building wings can be found built into later structures which occupy this part of the site - now in private ownership.

The remains of a portion of the north wing of the New House were excavated in 1990 and were found to be a basement level stables with a huge open central drain, and in the section excavated, stalls for sixteen horses.

To the west of the Old House is what has traditionally been known as the walled garden and has certainly been so since the 18th century, however, the purpose for its original construction is still open to conjecture. It is bounded on its north west side by the substantial remains of the original Tudor curtain wall which on its outer face has considerable diapered decoration and a series of musket and gun loops which have been blocked on the inner face. The wall is built with three facets, and in the middle of the outer face of the central facet the brick bonding and decoration is broken, indicating the position of a lost mural tower.

At each end of the curtain wall two multiangular towers still stand, both of which in recent centuries having served as dovecotes. However, upon closer examination the towers appear to have been originally half-decadel with their rear face flush with the curtain wall.

The southern tower of the pair has notable diapering whereas the north tower is plain but does have indications of having once been fenestrated and also heavily patched. Both towers show evidence of having roughly looped during the Civil War.

The Northern wall of the garden appears to have been built following the construction of the Basingstoke Canal, which destroyed the original curtain at this point and truncated the garden, leaving a small Tudor turret isolated on its north bank.

Finally, the southern boundary of the monument is formed by a unique set of earthworks dating from the 12th century but dramatically enlarged and altered in 1643/45. The original narrow southern outer bailey of the Norman Castle which appears to have defended the postern gate or sally port of the Old House was converted by Inigo Jones, and the Dutch military engineer, Van Derbline, into a rampier for the Old House. This rampier in turn was defended at each end by a raised gun platform which were protected by half moons to their fronts. The rampier itself has a broad salient angle which is defended by an eccentrically positioned four sided earthwork which may be the "Park Bastion" referred to in contemporary Civil War reports. This earthwork has suffered from archaeological digging on an underlying Romano - British building in the 1960's and still awaits restoration.

The Civil War defences on the western flank of the rampier have been obliterated in the present century with the exception of a short section of ditch. On the eastern flank of the rampier a large bank and ditch remain forming the southern limit of the New House platform although the date of the bank in its present form is uncertain. This flank is still covered by trees and dense scrub. The remaining earthwork which may be of Civil War date is a large angular flat topped mound to the south east of the New House. Early maps of the site indicate an angled corner bastion at this point but the surviving mound would appear to be much bigger and may have been enlarged by the addition of construction spoil from the Basingstoke Canal cutting which truncated this part of the site.

These 17th defences are in design unlike any other of the period in England and make them one of the nations most impressive surviving monuments to the Civil War.

Alan Turton
Site Manager
BASING HOUSE
1993

CONTENTS

Foreword By Brigadier Peter Young 4

Preface 6

Preface To Second Edition 9

Contents 14

Chronology 15

CHAPTER ONE: Setting the Stage 16

CHAPTER TWO: The House 23

CHAPTER THREE: Dramatis Personae 35

CHAPTER FOUR: Let Hostilities Commence 47

CHAPTER FIVE: The Lull before the Storm 73

CHAPTER SIX: The Ring of Fire 88

CHAPTER SEVEN: Disaster 114

CHAPTER EIGHT: Aftermath 128

BIBLIOGRAPHY: 134

APPENDIX: 139

CHRONOLOGY

1642

Aug. 22nd: Charles I raises Standard at Nottingham

Oct. 23rd: Battle of Edgehill (Marginal Royalist Victory)

Nov. 30th: Waller Takes Farnham Castle

1643

July 31st: First attack on Basing by Norton and Harvey

Sept. 20th: First Battle of Newbury (Marginal Parliament Victory)

Nov. 7th: Basing attacked by Waller

Nov. 15th: Basing relieved by Hopton

1644

March 29th: Battle of Cheriton (Parliament Victory)

June 6th: Cropredy Bridge (Royalist Victory)

July 11th: Norton's second attack

Sept. 11th: Relieved and provisioned by Gage

Sept 23rd: Norton reinvests House

Oct. 26th: 2nd Battle Newbury (Royalist Victory)

Nov. 20th: Gage relieves House

1645

June 14th: Battle of Naseby (Decisive Parliament Victory)

Aug. 20th: Dalbier arrives at Basing

Oct. 8th: Cromwell arrives at Basing

Oct. 14th: Basing House taken by storm

Oct. 15th: Demolition of the House ordered by Parliament

Chapter One

'SETTING THE STAGE'

How with Unhallowed Hands you strive to strike
Him who you should your loyalty afford
Great Charles the Anointed of the Lord.
                        Wm. Webb, 1643.

AT THE COMMENCEMENT of the Great Civil War, Sir William Waller wrote to his great friend, Sir Ralph Hopton, stating that he did not esteem him less because they had chosen opposite sides and finishing, "We are both on the stage and must act those parts assigned to us in this tragedy". The events leading up to the fall of Basing House have sufficient melodrama to provide adequate excuse to continue this theatrical theme. In Shakespeare's time a member of the cast came out onto the stage to proclaim the prologue, thus acquainting the audience with the background of the drama about to be unfolded. I will do likewise.

In the year 1642 when Charles I raised his standard at Nottingham and prepared to contest the issue with his rebellious Parliament, Basingstoke had achieved sufficient importance to have its first Mayor, one George Baynard. By present day standards the town would be considered a large village, for the manorial map of 1762 shows that even then it consisted of no more than the nucleus of the present town. The Whiteway (now Chapel Street) descended the hill from the Holy Ghost ruins to the valley of the infant Loddon where it met cross roads. That to the east was called North Brook Street, that to the west, Frog Lane. Alongside these two streets ran a small rivulet named Oliver's Brook which no doubt did

duty as an open sewer. The Whiteway ascended the opposite slope as Church Street and at the crest it was crossed by the High Street known then as now as Winchester Street and London Street. In London Street stood two taverns opposite one another, "The Bell", in whose basement was the cell where wrongdoers were kept, and "The Falcon", later known as "The Fleur de Lys". Amongst all the taverns in the town these are the only ones to appear in a later stage of our narrative. Church Street was paralleled by Oate (now Wote) Street, so called, they say, because the oat fields bordered it to one side. Coming in from the hamlet of Eastrop, now part of the town, but then quite distinct from it, was Haines Lane (now Goat Lane). Linking the two streets horizontally was Potters Lane (lost in the recent replanning of the Town Centre) Cross Street and Flaxfield Road leading into the Worting Road. Dwellings did no more than line the streets with great masses of gardens and open spaces in between while no doubt the focal point of the town was the Moot Hall which is shown on the map as a building raised on pillars at the junction of Oate Street, Church Street and the High Street. At least one exalted visitor found Basingstoke unprepossessing. The Grand Duke of Tuscany visited the town in 1669 and his secretary wrote, "His Highness walked on foot through the town, which is wretched, both in regard to the buildings the greater part of which are of wood, and the total absence of trade, so that the gratification of his curiosity did not compensate for the fatigue of walking even a few paces." We can only assume that this perfunctory inspection did not take place on a market day for the cattle market was of some consequence as we shall presently see. To accompany this account, the Duke's artist has left us a somewhat stylised sketch of the town as seen from the Holy Ghost ruins. The tower of St. Michael's Church is possibly all that may be familiar to a resident today, rising loftily above the surrounding low houses. The roofs are tinted grey and in others red so that we may assume that there was a proportion of the houses tiled in comparison with others thatched. If the traveller left the town by the "lower lane", that is along North Brook Street, and took the right hand fork (the other led to Reading) in about two miles along the marshy valley of the Loddon, he would be confronted by a scene of the utmost splendour. Before him was the great pile of Basing House with a forest of spires and pinnacles thrusting skyward over the high thick defensive walls of Tudor brick. Covering fourteen and one half acres, the greatest subject's house in the realm, it was the residence of the Premier Catholic Marquis of England — John Paulet. Its frowning ramparts commanded the main road from London to the West. John Ogilby's map of this road dated 1675, shows that it followed the route of the modern A.30 quite closely. In the confines of our stage or arena, we can see that it went through Newnham instead of Nateley Scures as at present and turning in the village to leave the church on its right crossed over the little River Lyde and rejoined the present road at the foot of Nateley Scures Hill continuing in the same line over Wellocks Hill where it passed close to Basing House going through Basingstoke, on to Andover and eventually to Lands End. Opposite the House was the Hawkwood or, as it is known today, Hackwood. At the time of which we speak the great house of the Dukes of Bolton did not exist. Instead there was on the site a hunting lodge built in the time of the first Elizabeth for the convenience of hawking parties. Eight miles to the east, just off the main road is a village we shall hear a lot of — Odiham. The description of it given by a combatant in 1644 seems to be appropriate today. He described it as "a single broad street with numerous accesses". Eight miles beyond it is the town of Farnham, a focal point of our drama, then as now nestling round the base of the hill on which stands the castle. The extent of the town in those days was probably along West Street as far as Potters Gate, along East Street as far as the "Seven Stars", along Downing Street as far as Lower Church Lane and from thence to the foot of the hill. The population at the time of the Civil War was about 1,000. The castle was an ecclesiastical residence from its beginning. Started by Henry de Blois, Bishop of Winchester and brother of King Stephen, in about 1138, the castle became a stronghold of some importance in the 13th century but with the Reformation it declined in significance and by the Civil War it had been out of use for some years, being maintained by a caretaker. Buck's view from the north face, published in the 18th century, shows strong walls and towers with massive buildings projecting high above them, majestic even in ruin. The Bishop's Palace where Sir William Waller made his headquarters during the years 1643-44 is a fascinating amalgam of buildings from Norman to Georgian, still in use as a college. It is open to the public at stated times and is well worth a visit.

Leaving Farnham by the great London to Southampton Road, Alton is reached in 9 miles. This also saw stirring events in the War, events that have a direct bearing on our narrative. Then a place of about 225 houses, we may presume a population of 1,125 persons, reckoning about five to a house. A rough estimation indeed but sufficiently accurate for our purposes. A map of 1666 shows us that the High Street then as now was the backbone of the town. The River Wey bisected it, having broadened itself out into the Cut Pond. It was spanned by the bridges of Cut Pond Lane and the High Street. The focal point of the town would seem to have been the market place which was flanked by these two streets and another called Nether Street. North of the High Street the houses were scattered. South of it the Church Lane led up toward the church of St. Lawrence, the scene of momentous happenings as will be shown. Church Lane was joined at an angle by Saint Lawrence's Lane and as they went past the church gates toward the cemetery they were called Holy Lane. Long before reaching the church the houses were again getting scattered.

Let us now go with our traveller to the Southernmost boundary of our stage, the ancient capital of England — Winchester. Enclosed by its ancient walls, of which only the West Gate and a small stretch of the wall remains today, the 2,750 inhabitants by no means crowded the area. Stukeley's "View of Winchester" c.1720, Buck's of a few years later, and Godson's plan of 1750 all show large open spaces devoted to gardens. The great cathedral begun by Bishop Walkelin in 1077 and completed by Bishop Fox in 1501, the final resting place of the Saxon Kings (whose remains had been transferred from the Saxon cathedral), King William Rufus and many famous Bishops and other notables, was to suffer dreadfully from the excesses of the Puritan sectarians: one can only be thankful that the building itself was spared for our delight and future generations. The castle, which appears in Speed's map as having two wards and many towers, was originally the residence of William I who constructed it adjacent to the west gate of the city. Milner[1] tells us it was about 850 feet in length north and south and 250 feet in breadth east and west, becoming narrower at its northern extremity where it was joined to the west gate. The keep was about 100 feet square and connected by a wall to the southern defences of the city. It was flanked by four towers one at each corner and another above the entrance facing north. The main gate faced west. Opposite, on the other side of the ditch, was a strong barbican in which a guard was posted: square towers at intervals looked down into the moat which was of varying depth but near the keep was said to be one hundred foot deep. A stronghold indeed!

The next place on our itinerary lies to the north, not to the ancient town of Newbury, which it may be worthwhile to record was half its present area with a population of almost 2,000 souls, but Donnington, two miles to the north of it on the road to Oxford. The castle here dated from 1385 when Sir Richard Abberbury received his "licence to crenellate" from Richard II. He chose a knoll on the highest part of a hill above the River Lambourne and adapted his building to the contour of the knoll. It was unusual as there was no keep, the disproportionately large gate house did duty as the strong point and is the only part of the castle remaining after its long siege during the Civil War, during which Sir John Boys defended it with heroism. Boys and Paulet at Basing depended on each other to keep the lines of communication open.

---

[1] Dr. Milner's "History of Winchester" Vol. 2 shows an engraving of two faces of the castle as a footnote to an illustration of the King's House.

Now our stage is almost ready to receive the characters that are to weave the robust, tragic and heroic fabric of our narrative. We come at last to Reading, sometimes hostile, sometimes friendly to the garrison of Basing House as it changed hands. Speed's map of 1610 shows us, as at Basingstoke, the nucleus of the existing town, but it is the largest and most important place we have yet considered as its population in 1600 was 4,700. The northern boundary was the present Friar Street which stretched from the Abbey to the Grey Friars Priory. Identifiable by position and by name is the present Broad Street (then spelt Brode Street); leading off can be seen London Street and St. Giles Street. The River Kennet flowed through the centre of the town in a series of channels so that in one place, just after what we now call St. Mary's Butts, there are "Seven Bridges". The map of the fortifications during the siege of 1643, the original of which is in the Bodleian Library, shows a most imposing system of bastions and redans ringing the town completely except in the south west where the Kennet has apparently created an area of impenetrable marsh for the map is labelled "Drowned Meadows". And now our stage is set. If the setting has seemed tedious then my excuse is that a stage without scenery or poorly furnished loses much of its audience appeal.

Chapter Two

'THE HOUSE'

The greatest subjects House in England. The Motto "Love Loyalty" was written on every window and was well practiced within.
Dr. Thomas Fuller 1644.

NO MODERN demolition contractor could have razed Basing House more effectively than Parliament's soldiers and the villagers after them. For centuries the House — probably the oldest manufactured and continuously occupied dwelling in Britain — had gathered buildings, fortifications and magnificence as a tree gathers rings until at the time of its destruction it covered 14 acres, second only in size to the great pile of the King's castle at Windsor. From the remains it would be possible to work out a plan by extensive excavation alone, but while the archaeologist could deduce the date of the structures and possibly their size from an examination of the foundations, an estimation of their magnificence would be in the realms of fantasy, was it not for the fortunate survival of several engravings from a number of different hands. When these are related to the archaeological evidence which has been gathered sporadically since the turn of the century the story of its growth from Iron Age earthwork to mighty palace fortress is laid bare.

Its beginning lies in those misty years before Christ when a typical circular earthen breastwork is supposed to have been thrown up by the Iron Age tribe known as the children of Basa, who have left their name to both the village of Basing and the town of Basingstoke. Surrounded on three sides by marshland it would have been in an ideal defensive position against the warfare of the times. We are able to prove occupation of the site during Roman times, as recent excavations of the site have turned up quantities of Roman roof tiles and pottery while Roman coins indicate an occupation up to the 5th century A.D. Still in existence is the Roman well discovered when excavations proceeded in 1904: this is 65 ft. deep with 17 ft. of water.

The next important stage in its development came with the Norman invasion. Adam de Porte, who had fought at Hastings, was given a large tract of land and chose Basing as his headquarters. He immediately started to fortify a position, a wise expedient in a land that was conquered only on the surface. He heightened and strengthened the earthwork ring and added an outer courtyard or bailey, digging a deep ditch all round and throwing the earth inward to form a hasty but effective wall. Adam, described by Camden as "a mighty man in this tract and of great wealth", matched his son William with the heiress to the "right noble house of St. John and to do honour to that name took upon himself the surname of St. John and they who have descended from him lineally have retained the same to this day". Thus we hear of the great moat being deepened and palisaded in 1261 by Robert de St. John who obtained a licence from King Henry III "to keep it so fortified during the King's pleasure". This ring and bailey was incorporated into the later fortress and can still be seen today, the bailey then as now protecting the entrance to the enceinte or earthwork.

After various transitions from name to name through the failure of male heirs, the estate passed in the reign of Henry VII by marriage to the Paulets, a Somersetshire family whose name will always be associated first and foremost with Basing House. It would seem that up to this time the House was little more than an unremarkable fortified manor with an accumulation of buildings from Saxon times onward. It is to the third Paulet, Sir William, that we owe its transformation into the palace fortress in which form it is best remembered. This gentleman had the enviable ability to tread the perilous tightrope of power and favour during the reigns of four Tudor sovereigns, and unlike so many other tightrope walkers he not only kept his head but accumulated vast wealth, influence and honour. Henry VIII, to whom he was Comptroller and Treasurer of the Household, created him Lord St. John of Basing.

It can well be imagined that Basing House had to keep step with the increasing importance of its owner. Here the engravings prove invaluable. They show the form of the mighty four storey gatehouse that he built blocking the entrance to the enceinte with a small tower at each corner, the bases of which are still visible, with a sloping tiled roof. The circular rampart was at this time strengthened by a red brick wall on the outside and the dry moat widened and deepened. From the top of the rampart to the bottom of the moat at the present time is 36 feet while the outside circumference of the moat is 600 yards. Round the upper rim a four foot wall guarded a sentry walk. This is still in existence but is in the process of sliding into the moat in great slabs. Following the contour of the rampart internally was a line of buildings which comprised bake houses, kitchens, store rooms, servants quarters and guard house. Two thirds of. the remaining space was occupied by a complex of buildings set around several courtyards. Entering through the gate house one stood in a fan shaped principle court. On the west side stood the great hall with kitchens, butteries, etc. on the north east. The ranges of buildings on each side of the gate house had cellars that under the hall being particularly commodious. South of the hall was a block which doubtless contained the principal living quarters, the great chamber overlooking a second court on the south east, while a third and smaller court of a regular rectangular shape was at a little distance to the south. There was a small court to the west of the Hall and another to the south east of the site, east of the rectangular court. The kitchen at the north west of the hall was an hexagonal building with large fireplaces in three of its sides and rooms at each side of it had ovens in the thickness of the wall and were undoubtedly bakehouses, while another room of the great hall shows remains of two large fireplaces set against the rampart and were probably a second kitchen. The Hall itself was of noble proportions and measuring 60 ft. by 25 ft. with screens at the north end and a north east porch and a shallow bay window at the south east. At the north end beyond the screens a broad flight of steps leading down into the cellar beneath the hall. On either side of the entrance to the cellar are rooms in the medieval position of buttery and pantry that toward the east having a bay window looking onto the principal court. A brick bridge led from the "Old House" (as we shall now refer to this portion contained in the enceinte) spanning the dry moat and leading into the Norman bailey, no longer staked and palisaded as in the early days but still following the ancient form. The hardness of the edges under one's feet where brickwork lies just under the turf bears out the engravings assertion that this was walled round and its surrounding dry ditch was crossed by a drawbridge protected by a small barbican, the brickwork of which is still visible. It was here that the garrison paraded. At the same time the "Old House" was being remodelled the giant New House the latest work in luxury and modernity at the time and reputed to contain 380 rooms was taking shape by the side of it. The east side of the ruins was much disturbed in the making of the Basingstoke Canal so that it is a moot point how far the New House actually extended, the foundations are only just now being uncovered. As this is of necessity painstakingly slow work it may be years before we know its full extent, but the engravings come to our rescue and show that it was part palace part fortress. The engravings, both by Hollar and by others which show the House (or houses according to your way of thought) both from the south west and from the north agree that it had a great tower in the north east corner with projecting turrets and another in the south west corner. It appears to have been five storeys high and was also surrounded by a deep dry moat. Four exterior chimney breasts are shown rising from ground level and ^projecting over the high tiled roof. On two sides it has a wall of no great height apparently enclosing a sentry walk. Hollars engraving appears to show it projecting through the Eastern wall to form part of the fortifications but this is not shown on the others. It is apparent from contemporary evidence that it was not a solid block of buildings but arranged round two courtyards and entered from the bailey by a great gate house integrated with the structure. Both Houses were enclosed by a common defensive wall nine feet thick, brick faced with an earthen core, with towers at appropriate intervals, almost a mile round. Only the north face exists today, but sufficient to be able to form an opinion of the whole. A close investigation of this wall is interesting if one has a mind to brave the coarse shoulder high vegetation growing before it. Pressed against the weathered Tudor brick the walls seem taller, almost unscaleable. In the brooding silence, cut off from the outside world by that huge forest of nettles, one becomes aware of an almost sinister spine tingling aura emanating from them and sight of the dark cannon embrasures in the towers and the dents in the wall itself where cannon balls have struck, makes one look shamefacedly over one's shoulder. The Garrison Gateway of which only the arched entrance still exists, still displays the weathered arms of the Paulets and is said by Prosser to have been erected in 1562. Curving out from the gate at this point is another wall which with a half ruined tower could be a flank protection for the gate. Examination of the weed choked site by the tower fails to prove whether it curved back on to the main wall or whether it went on as a secondary defence, as the whole slope is littered with half buried brick. It seems probable from the general direction of the wall that it did the latter. Amongst other things that make it obvious that the House and its defences were not designed to withstand the type of sustained attack that it was subjected to in the Civil War is the massive Corner tower. In a fortress this would have been a mighty strong point but is in fact a huge dove cote c.1530 still complete with the original revolving ladder gear and nest holes for 500 birds. No doubt they came in useful to supplement the diet of the garrison when rations got short during the siege and as Godwin dryly remarks "proved most useful with their heads down in the gravy and their legs up through the crust".

Inside the North front where the walls are furthest from the house, a triangular orchard and a garden are enclosed. The former, used as a cemetery during the siege, still yields an abundance of cooking apples but the latter is far from its original state, being just an expanse of rough grass yet it fascinates me above all else in the ruins by its potential past. Although I have no direct evidence to prove just what kind of garden it was, perhaps it is not too fanciful to suggest that this long irregular plot of about half an acre was laid out in a formal Tudor style and was the private retreat of William Paulet, created Marquis of Winchester by the boy king, Edward VI. A place where he could throw off the cares of state and walk solitary amongst the box edged fantastically shaped beds, the air fragrant with the smell of herbs and musk roses, allowing the peace of the place to restore his tranquillity of mind. Given this, it is a reasonable supposition that his short lived king also walked here when he visited the House, strolling there with the lady Marchioness, deep in conversation, possibly even declaring the country air suited his sickly lungs better than that of the town. One's thoughts can wander to the five day honeymoon of Mary Tudor and her husband, Philip of Spain, who came to Basing directly from their marriage in Winchester Cathedral. Can we believe that Paulet was entirely easy in his mind about the security of his position as he followed his sallow faced sovereign and her short limping husband along the paths? True he had been chiefly responsible for the Queen's tenure of the throne, but he had held office under two Protestant monarchs and Mary and her husband were staunch Catholics. Could he rely on her gratitude and appreciation of his abilities? If his mind was troubled on this occasion, we may be sure it was joyous at the visit of her successor and half-sister Elizabeth I in 1560. The Marquess was by now an old man of 85, as they walked in our beautiful garden. Elizabeth could be merciless to her foes, fickle to her favourites, but those who served her well, saw nothing but favour and affection. That she thought highly of Paulet is shown in her oft quoted teasing remark, "By my troth, if my Lord Treasurer were but a younger man I could find it in my heart to have him for a husband before any man in England". She was not destined to walk in the garden again until the fourth Marquess entertained her at Basing in 1601 when she herself was elderly.[2] On that occasion it is on record that "Her Majesty was attended on that night to Basing the home of the Lord Marquess, where she took much quiet content, as well with the state of the House as the honourable carriage of the worthy Lady Lucie Marquesse of Winchester that she stayed there thirteen days to the great charge (expense) of the said Lord Marquess". To add to the great expense the Queen received in audience the Due de Biron, the French ambassador, and his retinue, who were so numerous that they had to stay at the Vyne. What diplomatic secrets could have passed between the monarch and the ambassador in the seclusion of our garden whose stately formality lends itself so well to the occasion. But this is conjecture and we must return to proven facts.

The North front was partially covered by a large farm house known as the Grange. Enclosing this and its attendant huge barn and an open pasture was a high buttressed wall several bricks thick, capable of being defended. Godwin says that there were traces of brick foundations in the pasture, perhaps the remains of the store houses

---

[2] Queen Elizabeth Progress

known to have been fired in the siege, or the remnants of the dwelling built there in 1661, and burned down in 1704. Today while the wall still stands along the village street, only vestiges of the river front wall exists but here are the fish stews still, man made ponds where formerly fish for the Marquess' table were bred, but now used tor the growing of watercress. The farmhouse, barn and outbuildings still occupy the same position as on the engraving which shows the North front. The present house itself is not contemporary of course, but contains a profusion of fine oak beams, particularly in the main living room. But the barn, known locally as the "Bloody Barn", is said to be of pre siege date, if so, it is rather perplexing why it escaped the same fiery fate as the other buildings, but as a credential it bears the marks of the struggle along its huge loopholed length, the West end having a dent in it like a giant's punch, inflicted by a glancing blow from a heavy missile. The whole North front had natural defences as the Marquess' siege diary plainly shows.[3] "The Grange is severed (from the House) by a wall and a common road again divided from Cowdrays Down by meades, rivulets and a river running from Basingstoke, a mile distant". Marshes filled the valley here; the lower road from Basingstoke must have been mirey indeed.

The Southern face, which was the weakest militarily, looked on to a pleasant park, hence the modern Park Lane. Of the walls and towers that Hollars engraving portrays nothing remains, but a small rise up to a ridge proceeding in a straight line, now much overgrown, seems to mark their position, for the crest seems to have the hardness of masonry beneath it. Aerial photographs allied with the old

---

[3] Siege Diary

engravings are invaluable in piecing together the outer defences particularly those thrown up or improvised to serve the needs of the moment. It would appear that at first a bank was thrown up all along the Southern front and bastions added at later stages of the siege. Prom the air, details which are not discernible on the ground show up plainly and from these we can see that the central bastion had a five angled front while those at the South-Eastern and South-Western points were four angled. It is reasonable to suppose that the ditched bank continued on to the so called Basingstoke Bulwark on the North West corner of the defences proper. The Eastern face has been so completely destroyed by the cutting of the Basingstoke Canal in the 18th century, that all that is left is conjecture. The besiegers works were close to the defenders, as may be judged by Hollars engraving, but there is now no sign of them although O'Neill avers that in 1953 he observed a line of disturbed earth within a hundred feet of the Southern bastion, stretching for half a mile which in his view represents the Parliament works.[4] Cowdrays Down, unencumbered by the railway embankment as at present, was much favoured by the Parliament commanders being free of trees and offering a good field of fire for their artillery. An adjacent chalkpit, known as "Olivers Delve", was a convenient place to bivouac, affording good protection from the cannon fire from the House, and was visible until recently when it was obliterated by builders rubble. The Roundhead soldiers viewpoint is thus stated: "The place is very strongly fortified. The walls of the house are made thick and strong to bear out cannon bullets and the house built upright so that no man can command the roof. The windows are guarded by the outer walls . . . The house is

---

[4] Castles & Cannons

as large and spacious as the Tower of London and strongly walled about ... of such great thickness that it is able to dead the greatest cannon bullet, besides they have great store of both ammunition and victual to serve for supply a long time and in the wall divers pieces of ordnance about the House".[5]

It would not be well to close this survey of the House without mention of the church which served as a strong point for both sides at various times. This structure was very old at the time of the siege, the date of the original building (of which two arches survive) being 1089. The church tower, which was used as a lookout by the party in occupation, is of Norman origin with later brickwork. During the Civil War the church was gutted, its pulpit and pews burned, the Roundheads using it as a stable, as was their common practice. The exterior ornamentation is still badly defaced but two portrait busts appear on the South face of a bearded man and a beruffed lady, apparently of the Elizabethan period. It has been suggested that they are the first Marquess and his wife who built the South Chapel. Round patched holes and dents in the walls and bullet holes in the doors show how fierce the struggle was for this valuable strong point. Below the floor of the South Chapel is the tomb house of the Paulet family and their descendants. The names of 36 members of the family from 1682 to 1863 are contained on a brass mural tablet on the wall. The remains of earlier members were rudely ejected from their coffins by Parliament troops who used the lead to make bullets. The only members of the family entombed before the War who were left undisturbed are in stone tombs on either side of the altar, one of

---

[5] Soldiers Report

them, containing the mortal remains of that William, the first Marquess, to whom the House owed so much.

In siege warfare of any era the most unmilitary of structures often become vital key points and we can be sure that the barn that still stands adjacent to the church in Church Lane, built of the ruddy Tudor brick, had the double row of loopholes knocked into it on both sides and ends at short notice. For those who care to amuse themselves with guesses and suppositions it is an interesting exercise to try to fit into some sort of logical pattern such other odd fragments that remain. For instance, the small loopholed barn in Crown Lane, which is still standing, approximates to the far right where Hollar's engraving tells us the Parliament breastworks were. Could this have been used as a kind of command post? Did Waller himself plan his attacks there? Did it resound to the groans of Roundhead wounded? And what was the purpose of the tower almost opposite it whose base was uncovered recently during road widening? Perhaps the Park Entrance gate? But although we may allow our imagination to run a little wild on known facts, we must deal only with facts and leave surmises and suppositions to the writers of fiction.

Chapter Three

'DRAMATIS PERSONAE'

Now is a horrid tragedy begun, and still continues. Would to God it were done.
                                    Stephen Buckley 1643.

If we accept Shakespeare's statement that all the world's a stage and all the people players then the chief player in our drama must of necessity be John Paulet, Fifth Marquess of Winchester who was "on stage" for the entirety of the action. He was the third son of William, the fourth Marquis and Lucy daughter of Sir Thomas Cecil. On 7 December 1620 was elected Member of Parliament for the Cornish town of St. Ives. He became Baron St. John in 1624 and succeeded to the marquisate on 4 February 1629 also becoming keeper of Pamber Forest. Hollar's engraving of him shows a round faced man with the Van Dyke beard and long hair of the period with a kindly, even jovial, cast of features, but with a certain shrewdness in the eyes, together with a dogged set to the jaw and an imperious tilt to the head suggest that here was a man slow to draw his sword and even slower to sheath it once drawn: "Love Loyalty" was not only his family motto but the code by which he lived. His siege diary shows that he was inclined toward impartial neutrality in the beginning but was forced eventually to make a choice. It was unthinkable that he could choose any but the Royalist cause, although it is only fair to state in the words of Mudie "on the side of Charles the loyal men stood for the constitutional authority of the King" rather, perhaps, than the man himself.

A staunch Roman Catholic, his house became a rallying point for all the families of that religion in the South and caused Parliament newsheets to describe his garrison, "as a nest of Romanism , for they are Papists every one". Which like most generalities was certainly not true until the last phase of the siege. After the fall of Basing House on 14 October 1645 Paulet was committed to the Tower, on a charge of High Treason (18 October 1645) and his estates sequestrated (Commons journals iii 280/lv 313). An order was made that he should receive £5 weekly from his estate for his support. His wife joined him in the Tower on 31 January 1646 and the allowance was increased to £15 on her undertaking to bring up her children in the Protestant faith. On 30 June 1648 the Commons were requested to release him from imprisonment due to bad health, and in the following years the charge of high treason was dropped, but he was still imprisoned. After the restoration the Marquis received his lands back and although it was proposed in 1660 to compensate him £19,000 this was reduced to £10,000 and finally overlooked altogether.

Unlike others of the time who trimmed their sails to the prevailing winds and in the end emerged without loss or even with profit, Paulet's commitment was total, and in the end his loss was total. Total that is if honour counts for nothing. He retired to his estates in Englefield, Berks, which he had obtained by his second marriage and lived there quietly and privately until his death on 5 March 1675 devoting his time between agriculture and literature.

HONORIA, Marchioness of Winchester, was Paulet's second wife, the daughter of the Earl of St. Albans and Clanricaide. She bore him four sons (only two of whom reached manhood) and three daughters. Certainly he could not have desired a better partner during the siege, for she set an example to the garrison, casting bullets with her own hands, showering missiles from the walls on the luckless Roundheads that attacked the House, braving death every day. She went to Oxford to entreat for aid for her husband during Colonel Richard Norton's siege and was instrumental in securing Basing's eventual relief by Sir Henry Gage. She escaped from the House just before the fall and after the Restoration died at Englefield House in 1661 in her 52nd year.

SIR WILLIAM WALLER, the son of Sir Thomas Waller, Lieutenant of Dover and his wife Margaret, matriculated from Magdalen Hall, Oxford on 2 December 1612. Leaving university he became a soldier and fought in the Bohemian wars and took part in the English expedition for the defence of the Palatinate where he met Ralph Hopton and formed a lasting friendship.

On 20 June 1622 he was knighted and on the 21 November admitted to Grays Inn. In 1640 he was elected member for Andover. After early successes, notably the capture of Portsmouth, Parliament made him Sergeant Major General of the forces of Gloucester, Wiltshire and Somerset. In this capacity he took Malmesbury by storm (21 March 1643) and surprised the Welsh Army besieging Gloucester (24 March), he forced the Royalists to evacuate Chepstow, Monmouth and other garrisons on 25 April he captured Hereford. It seemed nothing could halt his run of successes when in June 1643 he was sent to contest the advance of Hopton from the

West. But he suffered a reverse at Lansdown which checked but did not halt him. By 9 July he had the Royalists cooped up in Devizes. They needed help critically and on 13 July a relief force from the King's headquarters at Oxford under Lord Wilmot met Waller at Roundway Down and defeated him.

On 4 November 1643 he was entrusted with the forces raised in Hampshire, Sussex, Surrey and Kent and with these defeated Crawford and Bolle at Alton also recapturing Arundel Castle on 6 January 1644. At the battle of Cheriton he dealt a heavy blow to Royalist hopes with his victory over Forth and Hopton. The self denying ordnance of 1645 robbed him of his commission and he never again took the field. When Cromwell and the army took over Government, he wished to challenge them with arms but no one was willing to take up arms against Oliver. Eventually he was confined to the Tower for his beliefs and released at the Restoration. He died at Osterley in 1668 and was buried in the New Chapel at Westminster.

SIR RALPH HOPTON (later Lord Hopton of Stratton 1643) was in the enviable position of being able to keep his personal feelings separate from his professional loyalties. His friendship with the Parliamentary general Sir William Waller was warm and enduring as their correspondence testifies but it did not prevent either from trying to outwit and outgeneral each other. At the beginning of the 30 years war Hopton entered the service of the Emperor Palatine and there received his apprenticeship in the arts of war. In 1624 he was lieutenant colonel of Sir Charles Rich's regiment raised in England for Mansfield's expedition.

At the coronation of Charles I on 2 February 1625 he was created a Knight of the Bath. He served as a member of Parliament for Bath, Somerset and Wells successively and when the quarrel between the King and Parliament was brewing, he at first supported the latter but later became a convinced Royalist.

In July 1642 Hopton accompanied the Marquis of Hereford to Somerset with the rank of Lieutenant General of Horse. On 5 July 1642 he was expelled from the House of Commons, and when the difference between the King and Parliament flared into open warfare on the 25th he and Hereford parted company, the latter transporting his infantry into Wales while Hopton with a small force retreated deep into Cornwall where with the aid of the local gentry they formed a small army of infantry. With these Hopton defeated a parliamentary force under Ruthven at Bradock Down on 19 January 1643. They were again successful in routing Lord Stamford at Stratton in May of that year and joining Prince Maurice's army at Chard on 4 June attacked Waller at Lansdown on 5 July and drove him from his position.

On 4 September 1643 Hopton was created Lord Hopton of Stratton as a reward for his services. Advancing into Sussex he took Arundel Castle but meeting with Waller head on at Cheriton near Alresford on 29 March 1644 was resoundingly defeated. In July Hopton met the King with part of the garrison of Bristol when Charles advanced to the West and was appointed General of the Ordnance. Succeeding Goring in command of the Western Army when the Royalist cause was lost, he met Parliamentary forces under Fairfax at Torrington (Devon) on 16 February 1646 where Hopton's army was shattered. Refusing to personally capitulate he escorted Prince Charles to Scilly and then to Jersey. He died in exile at Bruges in September 1652 aged fifty four.

SIR MARMADUKE RAWDON was born at Rawdon Brandesby near Guiseley, Yorks and at the age of 16 (1599) went to London apprenticed to Matthew Hall a Bordeaux merchant. In due course he went to France as Hall's factor and proving to be a shrewd business man became agent to other merchants and so advanced Hall's business and established his own credit that he returned to London in 1610 starting in trade on his own account. He became one of the most enterprising and successful of the merchant adventurers of his time, his transactions embracing most of the then known world, He imported wine from the Canaries where he founded a factory in Teneriffe, and traded largely in the wines of France, the Penninsular, and the Rhine. He was also one of the first to invest in sugar planting in Barbadoes. A fair example of the stature to which he raised himself is found in the fact that he owned or part owned four ships ranging from 80 tons (The George) to 300 tons (The Patience). It is hardly surprising that he was elected a member of the Municipal Corporation of the City of London and in 1639 an Alderman. In his leisure hours his recreations were the Red Regiment of the trained Bands (captain 1617, lieutenant colonel about 1639) the bowling green and billiards — then called tables. When the City began to side with Parliament, he went home to Hoddesdon House; which he built, and settled his affairs. Having taken leave of his wife (whom he never saw again) he presented himself to King Charles at Oxford, and Charles, who had been a frequent visitor at Hoddesdon, welcomed him and commissioned him Colonel. Rawdon raised a regiment of musketeers at his own expense which later formed a large part of the garrison of Basing House as we shall see. His Banner bore the device of a curious looking spotted animal[6] with a large bushy tail and elongated snout with the motto "Mallem mori quam tardari" — I'd rather die than stop my course.

On 28 December 1643 he was Knighted by the King at Oxford. In 1645 the Marquis of Winchester ill advisedly had all the protestants evicted from Basing House, and Rawdon became Governor of Farringdon Castle where worn out with fatigue and hardships he died on 28 April 1646 and was buried in the nave of Farringdon Church under a large black slab still visible. Accustomed as we are today to people commonly living into their eighties and nineties it seems curious that in the Marquis's diary so many references are made to Rawdon's "great age", when in fact he was only 64 years of age when he expired. The answer is of course that the average life expectancy in the 17th century was only about 48 years.

LIEUTENANT COLONEL THOMAS JOHNSON another Yorkshireman, born at Selby, was an apothecary in London. His shop was at Snow Hill and by diligent study and application to his art he became known far and wide for his skill as a herbalist. He became famous for his literary works on his chosen subject, his first works being published between 1620 and 1622, the best known being the amended edition of Gerards Herbal. His botanical expeditions led him far from home, even as far as Mount Snowdon. Like many others before and since, the war disrupted his life, and laying aside the pestle for the sword, he became Lieutenant Colonel to Sir Marmaduke Rawdon, being killed in a skirmish at Basing.

---

[6] Representing an Ermine.

SIR ROBERT PEAKE, print seller and Royalist was Lieutenant Colonel and Deputy Governor of Basing House throughout the siege. His father was sergeant painter to James I and probably responsible for many of the existing portraits of that monarch, while his portrait of Charles I hangs in the University Library of Cambridge. With this background it was hardly surprising that Peake and his brother William became engravers and print sellers in a shop near Holborn Conduit. When at the outbreak of the war he was commissioned into the King's service his enemies sneeringly called him a "seller of picture babies" but his services at Basing House, whence he came with a relief force of Sir Marmaduke Rawdon's musketeers, were rewarded on 27 March 1645 with a knighthood bestowed at Christ Church, Oxford. Taken prisoner at the intaking he was removed to London and committed first to Winchester House then to Aldersgate. He was subsequently released but refused to take an oath of allegiance to Cromwell. He eventually went back to his trade, being succeeded by his brother. After the restoration Peake was appointed Vice President and Leader of the Honourable Artillery Company under James Duke York. He died in July 1667 and was buried in St. Sepulchre's Church, Holborn.

COLONEL RICHARD NORTON came of a well known Hampshire family and resided at the Manor House, Old Alresford. The Nortons also resided at Southwick Park near Portsmouth and at Rotherfield. An ancestor of his was knighted by Queen Elizabeth I at Basing House. His association with Oliver Cromwell doubtless began when they were fellow Colonels in the Eastern Association; which ripened into a firm and lasting friendship. His bravery was acknowledged even by his enemies and his energy in pursuing the war can be judged by his persistence in pressing the siege. After the war he became Governor of Portsmouth, sat as a member of Parliament and was a member of the Council of State. With a nice turn of phrase we are told that he "dwindled ultimately into Royalism", at the Restoration.[7]

ROBERT DEVEREUX, Earl of Essex (1591-1646), Captain General of the Forces of Parliament, was the son of Queen Elizabeth's ambitious favourite, who had such a hold on the Queen that many of her ministers were afraid that she would marry him. His ambition was to land him on the scaffold in 1601, a proclaimed traitor. His son was restored by act of Parliament in 1604. He had seen service in Holland and in the Cadiz expedition in 1625. Carlyly describes him as "that slow going inarticulate, indignant, somewhat elephantine man", but while he might be biased against Essex there is no doubt that he was a lethargic, indifferent strategist. He was brilliant neither as administrator nor disciplinarian but was better as a tactician and had the affection of his men who were wont to greet him en masse by throwing up their hats and shouting "Hey for old Robin!" He detested Lord Manchester, one of his commanders, and hated Sir William Waller probably because of Waller's successful military career: a dislike which Waller, feeling that Essex had debarred him from higher command, reciprocated fully.

COLONEL SIR HENRY GAGE, who won golden opinions wherever he went, often to the chagrin of his superiors, was, we are told, "of a large and graceful person, and of honourable extraction".[8] He had seen service in Flanders and at the outbreak of hostilities

---

[7] Godwin

[8] Life of Gage

came to Oxford to serve the King. As he could speak several languages and had been much in foreign courts, he was looked upon highly by the Lords of the Council and given preferment above many others. From our narrative we shall see his quality and bemoan the fact that on 11 January 1645 he set out from Oxford, where he had succeeded Sir Arthur Aston as governor, with the intention of building a fort to keep the Parliament garrison of Abingdon, in check. On the way he was attacked by an enemy force and was mortally wounded.

WENCESLAS HOLLAR, whose engraving of the House during the siege was invaluable to me in reconstructing the plan and appearance of the place, was born in Prague in 1607. He was intended for a law practice but the fortunes of war which ruined his family, saw him installed instead as an engraver, and in 1636 by a fortunate chance became attached to the British embassy in Vienna. When the Ambassador, Thomas, Earl of Arundel, returned to England, Hollar went with him and obtained a post in the Royal Household. When the Civil War broke out, Hollar, in company with Peake and Faithorne, volunteered for the King's service into which they were commissioned. At the fall of Basing House he escaped abroad and returned at the Restoration. He lived in poverty most of his life, despite his skill at engraving and he died beseeching the bailiffs not to remove him to any prison but the grave.

WILLIAM FAITHORNE, the last of the trio of engravers who served at Basing, "the father of the English school of engravers", studied under Peake for two or three years prior to the outbreak of the Civil War. He served under him as an ensign at Basing and after its fall he was imprisoned at Aldersgate and was eventually allowed to retire to France. Returning in 1650, he set up in business as an engraver near Temple Bar and prospered exceedingly. He had not forgotten his old master and when, in 1662, he wrote his treatise on "The Art of Graving and Etching", he dedicated it to Peake.

MAJOR JOHN CUFAUD and LIEUTENANT FRANCIS CUFAUD, whose exploits we shall read of, were of an ancient family in the district, their name being perpetuated in the lane that stretches from the Chineham crossroad to Bramley. The remains of the moat surrounding their manor house is still discernible at the intersection of the lane and the private road to Vyne Lodge Farm. The scattering of houses in the vicinity are all that is left of the hamlet of Cufaud. The family were of very ancient lineage, and we are told that the Cufauds of the siege had both Tudor and Plantagenet royal blood. The name in the sources I have made use of is variously spelt Cuffles, Cufand and Cuffel. I have employed the modern spelling throughout.

COLONEL SIR ARTHUR HESELRIG, commander and founder of the famous cavalry regiment that were so completely armoured that the Royalists mockingly called them "lobsters", was one of the five members who were impeached by the King. It was Charles' invasion of the House of Commons to arrest these members that caused the final rift that led to the Civil War. He fought with distinction at Edgehill, Lansdowne, Roundway Down, and Cheriton. At the Restoration he was imprisoned in the Tower where he died in 1661.

COLONEL HARVEY, had been formerly a Captain in one of the regiments of the London Trained Bands. When the war broke out trained officers could expect quick promotion, and he was appointed to command a troop of horse and then a regiment of dragoons.

During the Commonwealth he became the owner of Fulham Palace and received various Church revenues, a happy state of affairs which terminated abruptly with the Restoration.

Considering the length of the operation, LIEUTENANT GENERAL OLIVER CROMWELL played a minor part in the siege arriving only for the grand finale. His rise to power from obscurity is too well known to need recounting here, but the general reader may not be aware that although many officers were Parliamentarian in allegiance, that did not of necessity make them Cromwellians. Many of them, particularly Waller, were as opposed to Cromwell's rule as they were to the King's. The portrait at the National Portrait Gallery shows him as having a long, hollowed cheeked face, with a high colour and a wispy moustache, a prim but not cruel mouth and commanding grey eyes, which with a determined chin gives the impression of a man who knew his own mind and who meant to get his own way.

Chapter Four

'LET HOSTILITIES COMMENCE'

*Behold I see the Blood of Captains both great
and small lie on the ground
Therefore strike up the drums alarum, let not
the trumpet cease to sound*

                        Wm. Starbucke, 1643.

IN THE YEAR 1641 affairs were coining to a head between Charles and his Parliament. Move and counter move, verbal thrust and parry followed quickly one on the other. On 4 January 1642, the pot boiled over when Charles made a monumental error of judgment. He entered the House of Commons at the head of a guard of soldiers intent on arresting his principal opponents, Pym, Hampden, Holies, Heselrig and Strode. No other King had ever dared to invade the privacy of the Commons before and the opinion of the London citizens was so much inflamed at this breach of privilege that they rioted against it, in fact so violently that Charles left London never to return except to die. It was the spark that ignited the powder keg. The Marquess of Winchester, who seems to have favoured a middle course, left his town residence as his diary tells us. "Hitherto, the rebellion having made houses of pleasure more unsafe the Marquess first retired hoping integrity and privacy might here have preserved his quiet but the source of the times villainy bearing down all before it, neither allowing neutrality or permitting peace to any less sinful than themselves, enforced him to stand on his guard".[9]

The strategic importance of Basing House had not escaped those Parliamentarians who, assuming the inevitability of a conflict with the King, were looking with a practical eye upon their potential enemies. Thus in the House on 19 August, 1641, "One, Mr. Lewer, did this day give information that he did see on Monday a great many arms in the Marquess of Winchester's house at Basingstoke, and that the keepers of them told him there were arms for a thousand five hundred men".[10] It indicates how great the Marquess's desire for neutrality was that when he received an order on 4 November, to dispose of the weapons, "to such tradesmen that will buy the same", he complied.

On 22 August, 1642, the King's standard was raised at Nottingham and the war began. Almost two months later to the day the first great battle was fought at Edgehill in Warwickshire, between the Royal Army and the Parliamentary forces under the Earl of Essex. There was no standing army at this time in this country and the only officers with field experience were those who had served abroad and there were insufficient of these. Hence, as Brigadier Young remarks, the campaign of 1642 was indeed fought by armies of amateurs.[11] After confused and bloody fighting, at least five thousand dead lay on the field, and the result was inconclusive. It was felt, however, that the King had the better of it as Essex withdrew to cover London. Charles

---

[9] Siege Diary

[10] House of Commons Journal

[11] Edgehill

followed leisurely only to refuse a further engagement at Turnham Green when he found that Essex had effected a juncture with the London Trained Bands. On 21 November, Lord Grandison's Regiment of horse and Colonel Grey's dragoons rode into Basingstoke and demanded quarters. A Regiment of horse was reckoned to be 500 men but often did not reach full strength, a dragoon troop was 100 men. Dragoons were mounted infantry, so called from the "dragons", or short muskets, which they carried. The town being of Parliamentary sympathy groaned heartily, as may be seen from a letter written by one "Master Goater" to his friend "a merchant of good quality in Lombard Street".[12] "They lay there eleven days and we had employment enough to provide meat and drink for them. It hath been a great charge to our town". Grandison also influenced or coerced a number of the Marquess's scanty garrison to join him before he set off in the direction of Marlborough.

In the luxury of his appartments in the New House, the Marquess of Winchester must have heard of the capture of Farnham Castle with some foreboding. Clarendon tells us that "Farnham Castle whither some gentlemen who were willing to appear for the King had repaired, was taken with less resistance than was seemly by Sir William Waller on November 30th".[13] John Vicars records exultingly, "That most noble and renowned Knight and most expert and courageous of commanders Sir William Waller with Colonel Fane and some others have assaulted Farnham Castle, within the space of three hours forced their approach so near to the Castle gates that with a petard they blew open one of them and most resourcefully

---

[12] Godwin

[13] Clarendon Book 6

made entrance thereto, whereupon the Cavaliers within threw their arms over the wall fell upon their knees crying for quarter which Sir William gave them".[14] Amongst the captives was the High Sheriff of Surrey and the booty consisted of £40,000 in coin and plate, besides all the arms and ammunition. On the best authority the pound in those days was the equivalent of £8.10.0., in modern currency, a great sum indeed.

Like rumblings of a distant storm, other disquieting news reached Basing. One by one other Cavalier bases which might have succoured the Marquess at need were falling. We left Lord Grandison on his way to Marlborough. This town was taken by the Lieut. General of Horse, Lord Wilmot, on Saturday, 5 December, 1642 after a short but sharp fight. After the fashion of the time, the town was pillaged. Vicars, who loses no opportunity to inflame public opinion, says, "Having obtained the town they most basely and barbarously pillaged and plundered the same and like so many traitorous and lustful bloody thieves ravished and abused the women and maids of the town". It was not to be thought that Waller would long leave this insult unavenged, almost on his doorstep. Very soon he was on his way to Marlborough. But the Royalists had evacuated the town, Lord Willmot returning to Oxford with "great store of armes, four pieces of cannon and a good quantity of ammunition". Clarendon states that Grandison through a miscarriage of orders was exposed at too great a distance from the Army and was forced to fall back on Winchester.[15] Godwin goes further and states that he was going to reinforce Basing House when he was cut off and had to retire

---

[14] Parliamentary Chronicle

[15] Clarendon Book 6

on Winchester. However, the Parliament forces coming to Marlborough, found the birds had flown and set off hot foot in pursuit, arriving in due time outside Winchester's walls.

Vicar's account of the storming of the city and eventual surrender of the Castle is understandably jubilant. Apparently the Cavaliers felt that they were ill-equipped for a siege, not having sufficient food to hold out for long, and therefore it was better to give battle and try for a favourable conclusion. If the figures given by Clarendon are correct, it must have been a desperate resolve for Grandison's force, numbered 300 horse and 200 dragoons, while their opponents numbered 5,000 horse and dragoons. So they marched out and formed a line of battle. The Parliament troops, still smarting from the indignity of Marlborough, were ready for a fight "and came up most bravely and resolutely to them and stoutly gave them the first charge with their horses and so there became a very hot skirmish between them for the time". Apparently there was fierce fighting for about 30 minutes: then the Cavaliers gave ground until they were safe back behind the walls again. Safe only for the minute, for the Roundheads, mad with battle lust were not to be cheated of their prey and scaled the walls. Brown's Regiment "notwithstanding the exceeding high and steep passage up the walls had of necessity to creep upon their hands and knees to the top which was as high as most houses, the enemy playing on them all the while with their muskets".[16] Eventually Brown's men did get up and "plyed their business so hotly and closely that they had soon made a great breach in the wall". The Cavaliers and townsfolk knew they had to hold the breach for their lives and the bullets flew so thick that none dared be first up.

---

[16] Vicars

Then Brown's Major, "a man of invincible valour", forced the breach into the town and the rest of his men followed through a hail of bullets and in their impetuous charge drove the Cavaliers before them into the Castle. With the wide ditch and moat they were virtually beyond the reach of their enemies, but the Castle, having no cannon, could not harm them. The Roundheads for their part had no cannon nor petards (which were a cone shaped explosive device for bursting open gates, fired by a fuse), but prepared a great pile of faggots and pitch barrels to burn a way in through the Castle gate. Meanwhile they ringed the Castle round with muskets and horse, so that "not a man of them could stir", and so they passed the night. Next morning, with no sign of any relief force, Lord Grandison negotiated, after some debate, the terms of surrender, which were in modern day terms unconditional.

Cornet Sterly. who was present, states that the officers taken were Colonel Lord Grandison, Sir Richard Willis, Sir John Smith, Major Hayborne, Captains Garret, Honeywood, Barty, Booth Brangling, Wren, Beckonhair, Lieutenants Williamson, Rogers, Elverton, Rodham. Booth. Cornets (in modern parlance second lieutenants) Bennett, Savage, Ruddry, Gwynn and Bradlines.[17] Some of the prisoners were sent to Portsmouth, others to the Lambeth House Prison. The Cavalier journal in reporting the event speaks in horrified tones (as well it might) of the pillage of the town, in particular of the Cathedral.[18] Apparently the rebel troops entered in through the great west door, colours flying, drums beating, weapons at the ready. The carved work and books were burned, the great organ ruined, but

---

[17] Letter Cornet Sterly to Major Alexander

[18] Mercurius Rusticus

when the tombs of the ancient West Saxon Kings and Queens were broken open and their bones scattered over the pavement, the horror of the citizens at this desecration overcame their fear of the Roundheads and such was the outcry that several of their commanders were concerned enough to restrain their men. Vicars, on the other hand, while not denying the wild sectarian excesses of the Parliament troops, merely says that by their spirited resistance during the attack, the citizens had brought it on themselves, "the town being full of Malignant Spirits" as he puts it.

While this was happening, Basing too saw action of a sort. Encouraged no little by the fall of Farnham and the weakening of the garrison by Grandison as we have seen, Parliamentary sympathisers launched assaults on the House.. Whether there were just a few snipers or a disorganised crowd, we do not know, but the Marquis notes that with "his gentlemen armed with six muskets" he stood them off.[19] Godwin suggests that this feeble sounding defence was probably backed up by showers of stones and bricks, thrown by the House servants. On 29 December, 1642, a tremendous explosion heralded the partial demolition of Farnham Castle, for what purpose it is difficult to say, for it was garrisoned by Parliament right to the end of the war.

The year 1643 commenced with a great deal of activity on the part of Parliament. The counties of Kent, Sussex, Surrey, and Hampshire entered into a pact to maintain and raise 3,000 foot and 300 horse for the service of Parliament, with Waller as Major General. Prince Rupert, the King's nephew, who at twenty-two had seen service in Germany, and had used his experience to create for his uncle a body

---

[19] Siege Diary

of horse that none of the Parliament side were able to equal, until the advent of the Ironsides, issued out of Oxford on 22 February with a considerable force to prevent Waller obtaining horses, arms and ammunition which he must have before moving against the Cavaliers in the West. Rupert reached Basingstoke and one can imagine that John Paulet welcomed him at Basing House, and received the latest information of the King's campaign plans. But his was a fleeting visit for action was imminent. On hearing of Rupert's presence, Waller had fallen back on Guildford. Advance parties of his troops had already penetrated to Alton and Winchester before his recall orders reached them. Rupert caught the Alton band, some 200 strong, on 22 February, just as they had tended their horses and were thinking only of rest and food after a hard day's ride. Seeing that the Cavaliers outnumbered them seven to one, they offered to surrender and, their offer being refused, turned at bay. They had a small field piece with them, a fact probably unknown to the King's men, and when the wild Cavalier riders charged their position en masse, the cannon vomited its load of musket bullets into their midst cutting a wide swathe of death through their ranks, leaving eighty dead on the ground. Although they often lacked discipline, Rupert's men never lacked courage, so they regrouped and charged again. This time they lost forty men. In the fast failing light they decided to wait until morning: no doubt reasoning that the Roundheads were like a mouse under a cat's paw. But in the morning they found the enemy, like the Arab, had folded his tents and stolen away. Warned by spies of a major attack contemplated by Waller and the Earl of Essex on Reading, Rupert fell back on that town and eventually withdrew completely to Oxford where the King had his headquarters, arriving there on March

28th. This left the way open for Waller's projected march on the West which he proceeded to carry out and hence marches out of the sphere of this narrative.

Although it was to be a year of triumph for the Royalist arms nationally, for the defenders of Basing the early months of 1643 were gloomy. One by one the Royalist garrisons in the district were being reduced, and soon it seemed they would be alone, then the whole fury of Parliament's power would be turned on them. This feeling of apprehension was deepened on 27 April, when Reading surrendered to the Lord General Essex after a twelve day siege. Farnham, Winchester, Reading gone, now Basing was surely in the lion's mouth. It must have become apparent to the Marquess that he could no longer conduct his own defence with the men at his disposal, so he made a journey to Oxford to petition the King to put a garrison into Basing House. Thus was Basing finally committed to a course that destined her to eventual destruction. Receiving promise of one hundred musketeers from Colonel Marmaduke Rawdon's Regiment, to be sent with all speed, he returned to the House on 31 July.

The Siege diary merely comments that they arrived with speed and secrecy and henceforth the place became a garrison, and that a few hours later Colonels Harvey and Norton attempted a surprise attack which was beaten off. But the Court Gazette Aulicus goes into more detail and states that Colonel Richard Norton hearing of the frailty of the House's defences and the richness of the contents decided to take it by storm.[20] Shortly after the Marquess's return Norton appeared, attended by Captain St. Barb with his troop of horse and Captain Cole with "a ragged rabble of dragoons" and breaking through the

---

[20] Mercurius Aulicus 31st week

park palings "begirt the house and pressed the siege exceeding hotly". The scanty six man garrison stood to on walls that Cromwell later estimated could only adequately be manned by 800. A pitiful gesture of defiance one might think. But in the tradition of all the best adventure stories help was at hand. Suddenly, unexpectedly there was a storm of musket shot. The troops from Oxford had arrived at the eleventh hour. The Parliament horse fell back before the vehemence of this attack and were cleared from the vicinity of the village and House. To complete their discomfiture further aid arrived at this juncture in the form of several troops of horse under the command of Colonel Sir Henry Bard. Discouraged by this sudden reversal, Norton's men retired hastily on Farnham. Bard had been detached by the King from the force about to march on Bristol when news reached him of Norton's intentions.

A note about the musketeers, of whom we have heard much and shall hear more, might not be amiss at this stage. The musketeer wore a leathern doublet, steel cap, cloth hose and square toed shoes with a large rosette. The description of the matchlock musket given by Wilkinson, shows the involved and time consuming method of loading and firing.[21] Simply, a length of cord soaked in saltpetre known as the match, which burned slowly, was used to ignite the priming powder which, in turn, ignited the charge. This match was attached to a device known as a serpentine, a double curved arm pivoted in the centre and secured to the side of the gun stock. First, however, the pan was filled with a fine priming powder. Then an exact measured amount of coarse powder was poured into the barrel. The shot was rammed home with the ramrod or scourer. Then one

---

[21] Guns p.24/25

end of the smouldering slow match was clipped to the serpentine and the musketeer blew on it to make it glow; it was then ready for firing. Pressure on the lower end of the serpentine caused the top end to move forward and down to place the glowing end on the touch hole. Defending a walled position or in enclosed or rough ground, well-led musketeers were of more value than pikemen, but in open ground they were something of a liability as the lengthy reloading procedure often precluded the possibility of another shot and the musketeer had either to shelter behind the pikemen or club his musket and close in under attack in these conditions. The musket itself was five feet tall and quite heavy so that it could not be held in the aiming position without a support. An ash stick with a forked metal arm was used to support the barrel. Not only did a musketeer have to carry his musket and rest but also his bandolier holding twelve little containers made of horn, wood or leather (sometimes known as the Twelve Apostles), a horn for priming powder, a bag for bullets and if he were fortunate, a sword. Imagine forced marching with a load like that! Musketeers were paid 8d. a day.

Hardly had Colonels Harvey and Norton been repulsed than the new men were set to work digging fortifications, to supplement the existing ones. Meanwhile, events began swinging back to the Royalist side in the locality. According to a 1773 history of Winchester,[22] Lord Grandison and some of his men were confined in Winchester Castle. The wily peer contrived to escape with two or three of his principal officers; one is named by Vicars as (Sergeant) Major Willis and they were received with great joy by the King at Oxford. Grandison then apparently persuaded Sir Will Ogle that

---

[22] See Bibliography. History ... of Winchester 1773

there was so few in the Parliament garrison that it could be easily retaken, and so it proved. Within three days Winchester was again held for the King. Ogle immediately set about strengthening the defences, the 1773 history telling the story graphically. "His first care was to strengthen his newly acquired garrison and render it as inaccessible as art could invent, widely considering that as its situation rendered it the principal key of the whole western county it might be made a serviceable rendezvous for his Royal Master...". Immediately after which the western army under Lord Hopton, marched into it consisting of 3,000 foot and 1,500 horse.

Parliament was becoming increasingly aware of the importance of reducing Basing House both from a monetary and strategic point of view. Patrols from the House commanded the main road from London to the West and trade was brought almost to a standstill by their activities in robbing the carters and clothiers that travelled along it. Fearing the intensification of enemy activities in the locality, other Royalist families had taken refuge in Basing House and had brought their plate and jewels with them for safekeeping until it was recorded "we having not less than seven score useless mouth within our walls".[23] The fact that the Marquess was reputed to be one of the richest men in the Kingdom, without the lure of this extra wealth, made the house a rich prize. Accordingly, Sir William Waller ordered his army to rendezvous at Windsor on 22 September, 1643.

But while Sir William was preparing fire and brimstone for Basing, things were happening on the broader stage of the national scene. The Earl of Essex, Parliament's Captain General, had set out to relieve Gloucester which had been under siege by King Charles

---

[23] Letter John Paulet to Secretary Nicholas

since 10 August. The city's governor, Edward Massey, was thought to be wavering in his allegiance to Parliament. Having secured Bristol, the royal army had only to win Gloucester and the River Severn would be open to the King, the loyal West would be united with Royalist Wales. But it was not to be. Whatever his personal feelings, Massey dared not, for his life, to go against the citizens who were Puritans to a man. Events rapidly moved up to a major battle. Brigadier Young succinctly sketches them in a table of events in this wise: 5 September the King raised the siege, 8 September Essex entered Gloucester, 15 September Essex surprised Cirencester, 18 September Rupert attacked Essex at Aldbourne Chase, 20 September the first battle of Newbury.[24] To fill in a little, Essex was en route to Reading, and to avoid the ring of strong points which surrounded Oxford he had to march to the Southward of them. Essex surprised 200 Royalists in their beds at Cirencester and seized 30 carts of bread and cheese there, a welcome addition to his men's rations. A clash with Rupert with 3,000 horse forced him to cross the River Kennet at Hungerford, and delayed him reaching Newbury. This detour was just sufficient to allow the King's army to block his way. On 20 September Essex moved into position at dawn occupying Round Hill and the valley below Wash Common with his line extending to the River Kennet facing the town. The Royalists attacked at 7 a.m. Like most of the Civil War battles, there was little finesse, but a toe to toe slogging match. Once again the Royalist cavalry under Rupert proved superior, but the Parliament musketeers and pikemen were immoveable. At nightfall a third of the combatants were casualties and the outcome was still undecided. Essex had no choice but to

---

[24] Hastings to Culloden, page 126

stand his ground and renew at dawn, but there was no need Charles ostensibly short of powder but probably stricken by the slaughter and the death of so many personal friends (for the loss amongst the Royalist nobles was high), withdrew. The way to London once more was open to the men of Parliament. Leaving them on their way, let us return to Waller and Basing.

In order that it should be understood, the composition of the forces that were presently to assail the Marquis and his garrison, the Parliament regiment contained 1,200 men beside officers. The Colonel's company consisted of 200 men, the Lieutenant Colonel's 160, the Sergeant Major's (modern Major) 140, while seven captains had command of 600 men. Each company had a captain, a lieutenant, an ensign (to carry the colour), two sergeants, 3 corporals and two drummers. One third were pikemen and the rest musketeers. Each troop of horse had in it 60 troopers, a saddler, farrier, two trumpeters besides a captain, a lieutenant, a cornet (who bore the troop standard) and a quartermaster. In the military circles of the day, there was some argument as to how many men were necessary to take Basing House, but Waller himself proved that he did not underestimate the Marquess's will and ability to resist when he ordered the London Trained Bands to meet him at Farnham. These Trained Bands were regiments maintained, trained and armed by a local authority for the defence of a city or locality. They owed allegiance only to the authority that paid them and were not responsible to any other, so that an agreement had to be reached before their services were available. The London Trained Bands had a high standard of discipline and although there was no national single colour uniform, they wore clothes of a single regimental hue (although their colours did not necessarily conform) thus they were often called the "Reds", "Yellows" and "Greens" because of this. Waller's plan of campaign was to execute a sweeping semi-circular motion from Farnham, occupying Odiham and Alton. Anything useful to the Basing garrison was to be totally destroyed in a forerunner of our modern "scorched earth" policy.

It is surprising how many contemporary accounts from the Civil War are still in existence, from officers, soldiers or even from civilians who took refuge in the anonymity of heading their reports "by an eye witness". Lieutenant Elias Archer in his, states that "On Tuesday, October 17th, the Tower Hamlets Auxiliaries marched from Wellclose, joining the other two bodies, the Greens and the Reds at Windsor.[25] By Monday, October 30th, they were on the move through Windsor Great Forest where they met by arrangement some of Waller's horse, his regiment of foot and a company of blue coats, "with snap-han muskets which guard the Artillery only; all these marched with us". It seems that after only an hour's rest at nightfall close to Bagshot they steadily advanced on Farnham, which they reached at two o'clock in the morning. Next day all the foot were drawn up in Farnham park, excepting only the Green regiment, which were quartered elsewhere, and was found to consist of 29 companies. On Friday, November 3rd, the regiments marched from Farnham toward Alton and were reviewed by Waller at Bentley Green. We are told that "the field state showed that there were 16 troops of horse, 8 companies of dragoons, 36 companies of foot and a train of Artillery consisting of ten heavy cannon and six cases of small drakes". Godwin surmises that the heavies were probably of a

---

[25] Archer's Account

type known as a demi-culverin which fired a 9 lb. ball with a 9 lb. charge of powder, with at least one demi-cannon throwing a 30 lb. shot with a 28 lb. charge of powder. Drakes were light field pieces which threw a 5 lb. shot with a 5 lb. charge. This last was a very useful "maid of all work" piece. All this great force was to crush a garrison of 400 men sheltering behind Basing's stout walls. That night Elias Archer's regiment was quartered in the little villages of East and West Worldham not far from Alton. November 5 saw the advance of the army on the road to Winchester, but this seems merely to have been a feint, for, toward evening, nine miles distant from that city, he wheeled back toward Basing, halting at Chilton Candover, midway between Alresford and Basingstoke. Hitherto, the Londoners had been quartered in barns and outhouses and failed to appreciate their open air camp site in the bitterly cold weather.

Like pieces being moved on a chess board, Lord Hopton fell back from Winchester to Andover and Salisbury before the menace of Waller's strength, while Ludovic Lindsey, 15th Earl of Crawford, with a large body of horse, advanced from Salisbury to aid the garrison. Dense fog blanketed both the approach road to Basing House and the site itself as the Roundheads advanced. It takes little imagination to conjure up a vision of a troubled garrison peering from the ramparts striving to pierce the thick white curtain that shrouded all the surroundings, while the rumble of cannons, neighing of horses, shouts of command and tramp of feet from all around told all too plainly the long awaited advent of the Parliamentary force. "But about one of the clock in the afternoon",[26] the mist thinned and shredded, then disappeared like a theatrical curtain as the sun grew

---

[26] Mercurius Aulicus 15 November

in strength, striking points of bright light from pike heads and swords and highlighting the colours of the Trained Bands' uniforms and flags. The Marquess himself went to the roof of the great gate house in the Old House to get a fair view of his opponents to assess their strength. Possibly he recognised and could even name the Parliament regiments by their colours, certainly Waller's colour with its distinctive device of a leafy tree from which depended a shield bearing the lilies of France with the motto "Fructus Virtutis" (the fruits of valour) would have been known to him. Having despatched the train of artillery and the army through Basingstoke to take up their positions on the slopes of Cowdrays Down, Waller sent a diversionary attack of 500 musketeers against the House. A detachment of the Tower Hamlets regiment under Captain William Archer advanced into a "little lane bordered with hedges toward the lower walls" which as the troops were still stationed in the park at this time can be conjectured at the modern Redbridge Lane, which connects the village street with the main London road.[27] These soldiers kept up a brisk fire of musketry until they had expended their ammunition and they were relieved by a regiment of dragoons. When the Parliament guns were in position they opened up with a shattering roar about four o'clock in the afternoon. After a dozen missiles had been fired, a parley was requested, at whose instance seems a little obscure, as Lieutenant Archer states that the garrison demanded it, but it seems more likely that Waller, having shown his strength desired to give the Marquess a chance to surrender before risking his men. The nature of Waller's ultimatum was as follows: "Sir William Waller, being present in person hath sent to demand the Castle for

---

[27] Archer's Account

the use of King and Parliament and he offers fair quarter to all those in the Castle".[28] Back came the answer from the Marquess couched in the defiant terms that one might expect: "I understand very well the words "King and Parliament" as they were now taken, but "the King" was one thing and "the King and Parliament" another. Basing is my own House which the law tells me I may keep against any man. That it is now more particularly guarded by His Majesty, who had put a garrison in it, beyond which command I know no obligation". Two hours later the chivalrous Waller again sent a drummer to the House offering free passage to the Marchioness and her children and all women and children staying there, an offer that was refused in a dignified but very definite answer. During the night there was a further bombardment during which 36 shots were fired at the House. There were now sited five sakers and one demi-cannon and the rest of the night was spent in constructing a protective breastwork, according to Lieutenant Archer.

Our martial ancestors apparently got little sleep on active service, for at daybreak on Tuesday, 7 November, the Roundhead batteries opened fire. According to Brigadier Young, the average rate of fire of cannon in those days was one round every seven minutes. The Royalist garrison took their own precautions by torching any cottages near enough to the House to provide cover for the besiegers. Meanwhile, Lord Crawford's horse was piling on all speed to come to the rescue of the garrison. Waller sent a strong detachment of horse to counter this move, being determined that none should lift the siege. About 9 a.m. an attack was launched on the North face which from the description in Aulicus was sent "down the hill", that is from

---

[28] Godwin

Cowdrays Down. One of the men in a letter later described the action thus: "We fought from ten to six, but two of our company was wounded. Never in the world was such desperate service on the very mouths of the cannon with so little loss".

It is as well to discount the losses said to have been sustained as the accounts are biased from whichever side they are written, but obviously the Parliament troops must have been sitting ducks in these frontal attacks. It is apparent that a general assault ensued on a broad front stretching from the grange to the church. Seventeenth-century artillerymen liked to fire at close range in order to inflict maximum damage, it is not surprising that three guns were brought to bear on the New House, which offered an excellent target, its great bulk protruding high above the encircling walls, unprotected by the circular earthen wall which surrounded the Old House or Castle as both sides called it. At this time to render this protection even more effective, all the rooms and other gate houses in the thickness of the earthwork surrounding the Old House, were bricked up leaving the great gate house as the only entry. It seems obvious that the Marquis intended this to be a last stronghold to be held if the New House and the walls were taken. But we can be sure his spirit ran high as he made his dispositions in consultation with the military governor, Sir Marmaduke Rawdon, who the King had ordered to join the garrison with the remainder of his regiment 140 strong and with the Lieutenant Governor, Lieutenant Colonel Sir Robert Peake, whose timely arrival routed the previous assault, as we have seen. Waller's captain-lieutenant Captain Clinson, described as "a man of great courage and resolution", took the grange by storm, "with very little loss, whence having steady aim at the holes and sighting from easy places, they much annoyed the garrison". All along the North face, the assault raged fiercely, the attackers being at a decided disadvantage by reason of the lack of cover. "Our Army had no shelter not so much as a hovel, nay not so very many trees, save only by the Park side, some few young groves which could not shelter us to any advantage .... yet did nothing to discourage their resolution".[29] Aulicus admits "that they took shelter in the ruins that remained from which they poured a well sustained fire of musketry, all the .while the guns battered away at the Castle and New House". The thick red brick walls were shrouded in a haze of powder smoke as the garrison went through the lengthy procedure of musket loading which gave them a firing rate of one every two minutes (vide Brigadier Young). Within close pistol shot of them were the Parliament foot taking advantage of every bit of cover, standing behind still smouldering walls and in their turn methodically loading and firing, spitting bullets down the barrel, then aiming at the smoke spouting loopholes, or, as a Royalist ball struck home, collapsing into the ashes, scattering dying embers.

The Grange, which was now carried, was found to contain ;'much provision of bread, beer, bacon, pork, milk, cream, pease, wheat, oats, hay and suchlike besides pigs and poultry and divers sort of household goods".[30] Now a strange impromptu banquet took place with cannon balls for grace and musket balls as hors d'oeuvres as one party sat down to eat and drink while their comrades continued the action. As one party became sated so another took its place and the first part kept up the attack. The assault was pressed so hard that

---

[29] Soldier's Report

[30] Archer's Account

they were soon hammering on the very gates of the House but Sir William failed to gain his prize, "by reason of the absence of his Grenadoes, petards and other engines to blow in the gates"[31] It would seem that the gates referred to would be the entrance we call the garrison gateway, not the great gatehouse in the castle as this would mean they had carried the walls, which we know was not so. The sight of Parliament's soldiers eating the food that was to have sustained the garrison through the winter, stirred the Cavaliers' ire to boiling point. Better to destroy the food than the enemy should gorge himself on it. Lieutenant Colonels Peake and Johnston decided that they would lead a sortie from the House and destroy the provisions. Colonel Rawdon, whose age might have excused him from such desperate work, but whose spirit burned with as fierce a flame as a young man's, joined that valiant band of heroes as they dashed forward on this suicidal mission. At once they came under heavy fire for the attack was still raging furiously all along the front. Desperate hand to hand fighting developed with no quarter asked or given. They fired the barns and outhouses while Lieut. Col. Johnston with 25 men penetrated "the very yard of the Grange".[32] Here the Parliament party's commander, Captain Clinson, met Lieut. Colonel Johnston in single combat. Had it been a film script the two armies would have ceased hostilities to watch this dramatic moment. But films were almost three hundred years in the future and this was grim reality. The Royalist soldiers had no intention of seeing Johnson die before their eyes so they came to his rescue. Clinson was overwhelmed by

---

[31] Mercurius Aulicus

[32] Mercurius Aulicus

weight of numbers and killed. Here again, Lieutenant Archer's account differs from the Cavaliers.

Although the contemporary accounts all bear out the basic facts, quite often they differ on details and it is difficult to ascertain just what did happen, for Archer states that Clinson was killed in an ambush, not in the yard and the whole story of the three most senior officers of the garrison leading such a desperate venture seems decidedly suspect. A commander said at a different time and place, "the next man can hardly make a true relation of the actions of him that is next to him; for in such a hurry and smoke as in a set field a man takes note of nothing but what relates to his own safety".[33] This may well be the truth of the matter plus a little journalistic wishful thinking.

About three o'clock in the afternoon the wind rose and it began to rain, dampening the musketeers powder and the men's spirits alike. The combination of the smoke and heat from the burning store houses and the foul weather "made the army sound a retreat which to give them content Sir William Waller retreated about half a mile to refresh them".[34] But all they retreated to was the discomfort of their billets in the fields where as Archer states, 'our lodging and our service did not agree, the one being so hot and the other so cold". Waller like the wise leader he was, instead of seeking shelter and warmth for himself in Basingstoke, set an example to his men by sleeping in the field on a truss of straw. After waiting in vain for the weather to abate, the following morning (Nov. 8th) he withdrew his sodden army to shelter at Basingstoke, the Vyne and other

---

[33] Royalist Official account of Edgehill

[34] Soldier's Report

intermediate places to dry themselves out. On Sunday November 12th, Waller returned to the attack like a wolf returning to a half gnawed bone. After an initial two hour bombardment, the Parliament army stormed it from all sides, about two o'clock in the afternoon giving in the words of Archer, "a hot and desperate charge". The main attack came from the North and North East and it was here that heavy masses of foot were stationed, 2,000 in all having as their objective the New House which had been selected as the weakest point militarily. Shouting their religious slogans, they poured all along the front and in places came so close to the walls that they were able to raise the ladders they had procured in Basingstoke. Again they reached the gate and successfully fixed and fired a petard. But the garrison foreseeing such an attempt had strongly barricaded the gate within and it was not shaken. It seems again probable that this was the Garrison Gateway as we are told that holes were knocked in a flanking wall by an "ingenious German" and a galling fire opened upon those at the gate, "whereupon the rebels lost heart and men as well".[35] Inside the House everyone took part in the desperate defence, even the Marchioness and her ladies, standing on the roofs of the out buildings showering down bricks and tiles and stones while Colonel Rawdon and the other officers did not scorn to fight alongside their men with muskets. Lieutenant Archer with the Tower Hamlets regiment and the Green Auxiliaries of London seem to have been with Waller's veterans in this attack. A newsheet commenting on this action says; "they hazarded themselves upon the very muzzles of the enemies muskets".[36] But the attack by 500 foot on the southern face

---

[35] Mercurius Aulicus

[36] True Informer

across the level open space of the park, was pressed with much less energy. The regiment is not named by Archer who probably did not wish to bring another local regiment into disrepute, although another source names them as the Westminster Auxiliaries.[37] Apparently they found that active service was a lot different from parade ground service and becoming confused opened fire before they came within range and totally forgot their drill. Instead of the front rank firing and then retiring to reload, allowing the other two ranks to come forward in succession, they all fired together, thus the rear rank fired on their own front and slew and wounded many of them. The incredulous garrison seizing this heaven sent opportunity, opened fire on them with case shot (tins filled with musket balls) and caused such terror amongst these untried soldiers that nothing could persuade them to advance again. The casualties sustained in this disorder was seventy men slain and wounded. Archer's comment is a masterpiece of understatement. "A lamentable spectacle" he wrote. The attack was carried on until it was too dark to see the loopholes then they were withdrawn to their cheerless quarters in the fields once again. There followed a night of heavy rain which further disheartened the raw soldiers of the Trained Bands. "The Complete Intelligencer" newsheet says; "The Trained Bands offered their lives to Sir William Waller in any service against men but were loth to venture further against walls, we must forgive them being young and raw soldiers". We may be sure that Waller who had shunned no danger himself and who had been unable to get the trained band officers up as far as his horses head held no such charitable opinions.[38]

---

[37] Parliament Scout

[38] Scottish Dove No. 6

About ten o'clock "the London Youths of the Auxiliary Regiment were sent toward the House to bring back the field pieces".[39] It must have been a thankless task creeping through the rain lashed gloom, trying to locate the pieces, fearful that any sudden noise might bring a murderous volley of case shot in their midst from the walls, stumbling and cursing over obstacles. Archer says that they achieved this "without incident" although "Aulicus" states that it cost them twenty lives. At this distance in time one must form one's own opinion, as I have stated before. Others of their comrades were engaged in the less hazardous but more morbid task of burying the dead.

The failure of this assault was blamed largely on the instability of the red coated Westminster troops. Waller was well pleased with the spirit of the Green coats, so much that he promoted their Captain Webb to be Sergeant Major and promised that their Lieutenant Master Everett should be made Captain at the next opportunity.[40]

On the following day, which apparently saw the rain turning to sleet and snow, the Parliament army again retired on Basingstoke to dry themselves out. On Tuesday November 14 there was a general alarm. Waller received notice that Lord Hopton at last gathering his forces from Salisbury, Malmesbury and Andover and disregarding or overcoming the pessimism of his followers who feared a repetition of the Royalist defeat at Newbury, was in motion toward Basing with at least 5,000 men. Archer says that his men were much encouraged that they were at last to come face to face with the enemy with no walls in between and Waller drew out into the open field to receive

---

[39] Certaine Information No. 44

[40] Remarkable Passages No. 3.

them. And as no Royalist army was seen all that day, the Roundhead army presently marched off toward Farnham Castle, quartering two miles away and then finally as there was still no skirmish arrived at Farnham at 2 p.m. next day. Despite Archer's insistence that the two armies had not made contact there is some evidence[41] that advanced Royalist scouting parties had indeed clashed with the Roundhead picquets which seems likely for Waller would have hardly have lifted the siege on a rumour. The Marquis of Winchester, understandably elated that he had again been saved, wrote that the only result of the nine day's blockade and fighting was the retreat of Waller "having dishonoured and bruised his army whereof abundance were lost, without the death of more than two in the garrison, and some little injury to the house by battery".

---

[41] Complete Intelligencer No. 4 states that Waller sent out some spies to lie in the woods to observe Hopton's approach and report on their numbers.

Chapter Five

'THE LULL BEFORE THE STORM'

"This only will we say, some of both sides did extremely well, and others did as ill and deserved to be hanged".

Parliamentary Commander's Report.

LORD HOPTON'S arrival was something of an anticlimax for anyone that expected a fiery and bloody end to the meeting of his lordship and Waller. The day after the Parliament General had made his retreat on Farnham, Hopton made his headquarters at Odiham. On the 17 November, he visited the Marquess at Basing and his men helped further to fortify the House.[42] An old but favoured aunt of mine had a large print in her dining room, I recall, that fascinated me as a child. It was of the relief of Ladysmith in the Boer War. In it a lean, heavily moustached officer leading the relief force was shaking hands with the garrison commander. Each had a sombre, stiff upper lip expression on their faces. But their men were not ashamed to show their feelings. Standing in front of their tents they were cheering themselves hoarse, waving their helmets in an excess of relief that they no longer needed to fear the besiegers. Although Ladysmith and Basing were two and a half centuries apart it is thus that I like to visualise the meeting of Hopton and Paulet: the former leaning down from his horse to grasp the Loyal

---

[42] Siege Diary

Marquess's hand and the garrison cheering themselves hoarse. But the expected battle did not materialise, even although the two armies faced each other on a heath outside Farnham. It is presumed that Hopton hesitated to contest the issue because he was uncertain of Waller's strength and Waller because he knew that his strength was considerably less than Hopton's![43] And so the two contestants behaved like two fighting bulls, pawing up the ground and bellowing, yet neither wishing to charge. Skirmishes on a smaller or greater scale took place all round the surrounding area until, on Thursday, 30 November, Hopton withdrew his outposts from Odiham, Basingstoke and Long Sutton and withdrew to Winchester.[44] Lord Crawford with his cavalry quartered at Alton.

Meanwhile with the strange ebb and flow of army strength that was common in those days, but which seems strange to us who are used to having a Regular Army, Waller had been reinforced from London. On 16 November, all the horse of Waller's great friend, Sir Arthur Heslerig — whose banner bore an anchor dangling from the clouds with "Only in Heaven" as a motto — were commanded to parade next day ready to join Waller at Farnham. Clarendon writes of these famous troopers thus: "A fresh regiment of horse, which were so completely armoured that they were called by the other side, the regiment of lobsters, because of their bright iron shells with which they were covered, being perfect cuirassiers and were the first to be so armed on either side". By Monday, 20 November, they were en route for Farnham. At first the regiment of Kent had refused to

---

[43] Kingdoms Weekly Post No. 3.

[44] Scottish Dove No. 6.

march until their arrears of pay had been settled, but, upon a promise that they would be paid at Farnham, they marched and arrived at Waller's headquarters on Tuesday, 21 November. Later the same day, Colonel Richard Norton arrived with his famous corps known as the "Hambledon Boys". With the arrival of these welcome reinforcements, the Parliament forces again numbered 4,000 — a formidable force. Lieutenant Archer tells us that on 23 November, "there came to us ... out of Kent a very fair company of horse and a company of dragoons consisting of 120 under the command of Sir Miles Livesay". The Kentish men got their pay, for one Alderman Towse advanced £2,000 immediately in consideration of interest paid at eight per cent.[45]

But, as we have seen, all this accession of strength was not intended to be dissipated in fruitless skirmishing. No doubt Basing thought soon to have the whole crew round about their necks again, but Waller had larger fish to fry than the Marquess and his stout hearted garrison. After a personal visit to London to obtain even more reinforcements, supplies and finance, on 9 December, 1643, the Parliament force was ready to move toward their ultimate destination, Arundel Castle, their immediate aim being the reduction of Alton, which, as we have seen, was where Lord Crawford and his horse lay 500 strong. With him was an infantry regiment commanded by Colonel Richard Bolle about 1,300 strong drawn from the garrison of Wallingford. The Parliament Army made as if to go to Basing House but, as Lieutenant Archer says, "after marching that way two miles we turned to the left and marched in a remote way between wood and hills marched beyond Alton and about nine of the

---

[45] Godwin

clock on Wednesday morning December 18th, came upon the West side of the town", without attracting attention.[46] Even Mercurius Aulicus admits that Royalists were taken by surprise. "Our scouts had concentrated their attention on the main road, not expecting an attack from any other quarter". Shortly Lord Crawford was seen to be galloping out of the town with his troopers hot foot to Winchester, "promising to send back reinforcements". Soon the combatants were treated to the extraordinary sight of Crawford galloping back again.[47] But it was not a change of heart on his part. Leaving Alton by the Easterly route, he had found his way blocked by Heslerig's "Lobsters", and turning tail galloped back again on the direct route to Winchester with the shining figures of the armour clad squadrons in hot pursuit. Lieutenant Archer gives a very full and precise account of the fight that followed as the gallant men of Bolle's command, outnumbered four to one, prepared to sell their lives dearly, but space permits only a condensed version. Archer says: "Now was the enemy constrained to partake himself and all his forces to the church, churchyard and one great work on the North side of the church all which they kept near upon two hours very stoutly and having made scaffolds in the church to fire out the windows fired very thick from every side".[48] Absence of a standard uniform made a password necessary to tell friend from foe. The Cavalier word was "Charles", the Parliament "Truth and Victory". Eventually the Royalists retired wholly back into the Church where they hoped to hold out until the promised relief arrived. But the

---

[46] Also confirmed by Waller's Dispatch

[47] Waller's Dispatch

[48] Archers Account also includes in taking of Alton

enemy followed them so closely that they had no time to barricade the door. Led by a Major Shambrooke, the Parliamentarians forced an entry striking out with their halberds, swords and musket stocks. At this critical point Bolle strove to rally his men, shouting "God damn my soul if I do not run my sword through the heart of the first man that asks for quarter". But after a short resistance during which many were killed the soldiers threw down their arms and asked for quarter which was granted them. But Colonel Bolles would have none of it and mounted into the pulpit where traditionally he was killed. Archer comments: "He being slain they all yielded and desired quarter. Being subdued all the prisoners were put in a great barn adjoining the Churchyard". The high esteem in which Bolle was held by the Royalist command can be seen in this letter to Sir William Waller from his great friend and opponent. Lord Hopton. "To Sir W. Waller — Sir — This is the first evident ill success I have had. I must acknowledge that I have lost many brave and gallant men, I desire you, if Colonel Bolles be alive, to propound a fit exchange. If dead that you will send me his corpse. I pray you send me a list of such prisoners as you have, that such choice men as they are may not continue long unredeemed. God give a sudden stop to this issue of English blood which is the desire, Sir, of your faithful friend to serve you. Ralph Hopton, Winton 16th December".

Having triumphed, Waller prepared to march on to Arundel but as Archer naively explains the Trained Bands wanted to be home for Christmas so they asked Waller for their discharge and as he had only had them on a temporary loan basis he was forced to let them go.

The story of Basing House here takes a definite cloak and dagger slant. With all quiet around him, the Marquess began to feel uneasy.

Were the enemy really preoccupied or were they trying to lull him into a state of false security only to strike when he least expected it? He became anxious for a little inside information and decided to send a spy into London to obtain the latest intelligence of the movement of the Parliament armies. He chose Tobias Baisley, who was employed to make bullets in the house for 5/- a week and all found. But Tobias ventured once too often to the City on these errands. Mercurius Civicus, from whose columns this sad story is taken, relates that Tobias was eventually apprehended as a spy. "A Council of Warre" assembled on 6 February, 1644 and the accused was found guilty and condemned. Twelve days later he was taken to Smithfield "Guarded by Mr. Quartermain, the Marshal, and divers others of the City Officers, and a company of the trained bands", and the writer exclaims with some surprise that when the executioner came to do his office the victim "showed much unwillingness to go off the ladder".

As we have seen, Sir William Waller had the greatest personal regard for his friend Lord Hopton, a regard which was reciprocated, but professionally both men were continually striving to be top dog. The bane of every commander's life at this stage of the war was the loss of numbers by desertion. Both sides were impressing men into the army, and these deserted at the first available opportunity. On 27 February, of 600 men who had been forced into the ranks by Hopton, 100 deserted at once and 200 more were missing before the detachment reached Winchester, despite the deterrent of a guard of horse. One thousand men were also said to have deserted Waller at the siege of Basing. Waller, having returned after the capture of Arundel Castle and his success at Alton was again massing men at

Farnham. His difficulties were manifold. One thousand horse under Sir William Balfour, which had been lent to him grudgingly by the Earl of Essex, might be recalled at any time. The Auxiliary Regiments of London were getting restless, as their period of service was almost up. On 23 February, a Captain Guthred "and some others", went over to the Cavaliers. Lord Hopton had his troubles also. On 1 March, 1644 he had less than 6,000 men at Winchester, which number was daily reduced by deserters. Nothing further from a state of readiness for battle could be imagined, yet within the month one of the most decisive battles ever fought on Hampshire soil was to be enacted, which, as the King's secretary, Edward Walker, wrote, "necessitated his Majesty to alter the scheme of his affairs and in the place of an offensive to make a defensive war".

The heavy snow of the winter 1643/4 had terminated hostilities for a period but now the two commanders were nothing loth to settle matters between them, not only on a national but a personal basis. Waller was still smarting from the defeats at Lansdowne and Roundway Down inflicted by Hopton in the early part of 1643, while Clarendon states with reference to the loss of Bolle's regiment at Alton that "The Lord Hopton sustained the loss of that regiment with extraordinary trouble of mind and as a wound that would bleed inward, and therefore was that more inflamed with desire of a battle with Waller to make even all accounts". The Parliament Army consisted of the London Brigade, which was composed of the White, Red, and Southwark Regiments under Major General Browne, the Kentish force under Sir Michael Livesey, and the horse, which included the famed Heselrig's "Lobsters", under the command of Sir William Balfour. Colonel Harvey, who, it will be remembered, was repulsed at Basing, had also been ordered with his regiment to support Waller. Lord Hopton and his firm friend and superior officer, Lord Forth, commanded the Royalist Army, which was composed of about 10,000 men. In the first instance Waller drew up his men on the high wooded ground between East and West Meon facing towards the South.[49] The Cavaliers occupied Old Winchester Hill, whose earthen ramparts tell us that it was no stranger to martial manoeuvres. Waller, decided to fall back on Alresford as a strategic move to cut Hopton off from his base at Winchester. In order to keep his army together as one unit as they withdrew, the Parliament horse were ordered to keep the same pace as the foot, making the withdrawal naturally slow. But Hopton, when he perceived the move and realised his opponent's purpose, sent his cavalry and dragoons ahead and blocked Waller's move by seizing Alresford. As the two armies manoeuvred for position, the Royalists took Tichborne Down anticipating a Roundhead retreat. But Waller was eager to fight and picked a position along the line of the present Cheriton to West Meon road where his musketeers had the benefit of thick hedges to shelter behind. Three blocks of cavalry occupied his centre and the village of Hinton Ampner was at his back. The Royalist forces were drawn up between Alresford and Waller, occupying the East Down which dominated Waller's right. The battle field is described thus: "The position occupied by each army was strong, the ground rapidly descending in front of the Parliamentarians formed a regular escarpment and before the Royalists it was equally but more irregularly steep while the wood with detached hedges and copses

---

[49] I have used "Roundhead General" as main authority for Cheriton

lay between".[50] Perhaps to over simplify the battle: Lord Forth sent out a regiment of foot and horse to take Hinton Ampner in Parliament's rear, and in the manner of a chess player putting a pawn to protect a knight, ordered Colonel Bard to take his regiment to cover their retreat. But the waiting game did not suit Bard who charged on into the battle for the village, opening up a great gap between the attacking force and the main army. The inevitable happened, the parliament cavalry crushed both regiments and their foot retook the village. Making use of every inch of cover, the Roundhead musketeers on the right slowly made headway up through the woods on the lower part of East Down where cavalry could not operate while their left reformed and began to put pressure on the Royalist right. Clarendon says: "the foot regiments on both sides fought stoutly and came up to push of pike. The London forces and the Kentish men under Waller did brave service". It was not good cavalry country, however, for a Parliament writer remarks that "the ground where the enemy horse stood was so broken and uneven that it could not march in any order". Steadily the two wings of the Roundheads were closing in on the Royalist flanks. At this juncture, Lord Forth poured in his cavalry who charged but were thrown into disorder by the narrow bottleneck of Scrubs Barn Lane. The Roundhead cavalry in the centre stood firm all through that long bloody and hard fought afternoon as Forth threw all but one of his regiments at them, 2,000 men in all. As Wellington said after Waterloo, "It was a close run thing", and perhaps more topically a Roundhead officer stated that at one stage "the day was doubtful if not desperate". The Cavaliers' very gallantry became their undoing.

---

[50] Godwin

In their eyes there was only one place for their officers and that was at the front of the squadron, only one possible command and that was "attack". By four in the afternoon so many commanders had been lost that the men were almost leaderless. Now Major General Browne collected 100 musketeers from the hedges and poured a heavy volley into the wavering but not yet routed Cavalier cavalry. They started to wheel and "a hot charge from our horse forced them to a disorderly retreat".[51] 500 Parliament musketeers now left the shelter of the hedges and advanced at speed so that the Royalist foot "who had stood to it all day, perceiving their horse begin to fly, do seek shelter by flight themselves and to throw away their arms". Another charge by Balfour's horse, including the "Lobsters" who had been discomfited early in the day, completed the work. According to local tradition, the lane from Sutton Scrubbs to Cheriton ran red with blood as the Kentish men slaughtered without mercy the red coated Irish men of Inchiquin's Regiment, who were the first of the King's men to break. Lord Hopton himself strove valiantly to cover the retreating infantry with a cavalry shield composed of the regiments of Colonels Butler, Neville and Howard. The "Lobsters" and Balfour's men were energetic in pursuit and succeeded after a chase of three or four miles in catching up with the retreating infantry. According to a local tradition the foot shouted to the cavalry remnants "Face them for God's sake, face them once more!" The gallant cavalry faced about. Across the fields could be seen the standards and the glittering menace of Heslerig's men. The battle-worn cavaliers on their jaded horses formed line and drew their blood-stained swords,. Some nameless but valiant officer, gave the

---

[51] Balfours Dispatch

order to charge.-With cries of "Charles and the Cause"! that heroic band hurled themselves on to their opponents only to break like a wave against a breakwater. It was five o'clock before the battle ended.

Sometimes these ancestors of ours seem iron men, inured to fatigue, discomfort, and even death. But that they were only human like ourselves is shown when Sir William Balfour, the Parliament cavalry leader, delayed writing his report on the battle to the House of Commons until the next day. His stated reason being that after the battle and the pursuit of the Royalists to within four miles of Winchester he was so desperate for sleep that he had postponed it. But what happened to milords Hopton and Forth? Hopton "with his horses and carriages, it being night, wheeled about through a narrow lane and so went unperceived" to the garrison of Basing House. With him went the Earl of Forth and fourteen other officers. Godwin says that their line of retreat was via Avington (presumably meaning Ovington) with a considerable body of troops which reached Basing in good order. The slaughter at Cheriton was heavy, a reliable estimate giving the Royalist casualties at 1,400 and Parliament's as 900. The number of Royalist "gentlemen of quality" slain is said to have been four hundred and eighty five. Lord Hopton must have felt very keenly the difference between his last visit and his present one as weary and dejected he came into Basing House and told the whole tragic story to his host and his senior officers. But he was not a man to be long idle, for on Sunday, 31 March, leaving his wounded behind him, he proceeded on his way to Oxford where he had the unpleasant task of reporting his defeat to the King. One wonders just what sort of reception he got. Waller must have been elated that for once he had no Cavalier army countering him, no Hopton to breathe down his neck, the only ones hostile to his cause and himself scattered or immovable behind walls.

The London Brigade halted at Alresford which had been put to the torch as the Cavaliers had retreated from it. So close had been the pursuers that the flames had been extinguished before they had properly caught hold and only a very few houses had been made untenable. Major General Browne their commander was resting there while the indefatigable Waller marched on Winchester, where he found that most of the Cavaliers had retreated on Andover leaving just one hundred musketeers to hold the castle. If he felt that the victory at Cheriton would ensure that he would gain possession of the castle, he was mistaken. The gates remain stubbornly shut. Not so the city gates, however. The Mayor and Corporation came out in solemn procession to give him the keys, "declaring their adherence to King and Parliament" and desiring to be saved from violence and pillage, which they were accordingly.[52] Merely staying there long enough to rest and refresh his men, Waller hastened after the retreating Cavaliers to Salisbury and thence out of the area which concerns us here.

The garrison of Basing House were much cheered in the following months by the presence amongst them of Dr. Thomas Fuller who had been acting as Hopton's Chaplain. A man of an observant and literary turn of mind, he made observations of local conditions wherever the service took him and wrote of the "troutful streams" and "natural commodoties" of Hampshire and in particular of Basing House thus: "Basing, built by the first Marquess of Winchester was the greatest

---

[52] Godwin

subjects house in England ... the motto 'Love Loyalty' was written on every window thereof and was well practised within".

We may be sure that with the accounts of the defeat of Cheriton, the spirit of the loyal Marquess, Sir Marmaduke Rawdon, and Sir Robert Peake flamed that much higher. But for a number of the garrison it seemed that with Cheriton the writing was on the wall, chief amongst these defeatists being the Marquess's brother, Lord Edward Paulet. He headed a plot to treat with Waller and deliver, the House into his hands. There is no evidence that his was a traitorous nature. His reason was probably the valid one, that to fight on meant only the destruction of the House and all in it. Possibly he reasoned that his brother must be saved from his own folly, by force if necessary. But, however, sound his reasoning, he had forgotten the family motto "Love Loyalty" and that was eventually to cost him dear. Only by the merest chance was the plot discovered, Sir Richard Grenville, an Irish officer, had come over from Ireland to serve the King. Captured at Liverpool he then offered his sword to Parliament and served under Waller through the winter of 43/44, becoming one of his principal officers. Early in March 1644 Grenville again changed sides and rode to the King at Oxford with 30 troopers, £600 of Parliament's money, and a magnificent coach and six. The plot was revealed to the King, who immediately sent an urgent dispatch to Basing. The incredulity, disillusion, and finally anger of the Marquess does not need to be guessed at, for after obtaining confessions from his brother and his accomplices "regarding all the circumstances of the correspondence and combination", he asked the King that his brother might be spared after justice had been done on the others. His punishment of Lord Edward was of a particularly sadistic sort. He appointed him garrison hangman; not only to had he to hang his fellow conspirators but all future malefactors too. On the list of prisoners taken at Basing House when it fell, we find his name, "Edward Paulet — hangman".

Meanwhile Waller and Essex were vigorously recruiting yet again to fill the gaps left by disease, desertions, battle and more particularly the departure for home of the London and Kentish auxiliaries. The Earl of Essex's army was to consist of 7,500 men besides officers, making seven regiments. £1,700 was voted for powder for it alone. It was no wonder that with all these activities and beating of the drum going on from Waller's headquarters at Farnham and Essex's at St. Albans, the King should be preparing for whatever campaign was planned. About the middle of April the King mustered an army in person at Marlborough, consisting of 6,000 foot and more than 4,000 horse in case Waller marched again into the West country. When he discovered that the preparations continued unabated without any sign of imminent departure, he advanced to Newbury to be near at hand if Wallingford, etc., was threatened. But if Basing thought that they were forgotten with all this portentous activity they were rudely disillusioned when on Wednesday, 24 April Sir William Waller "hearing of a large convoy of provisions and much cattle destined for Basing House" sent out a party of horse who intercepted it, and captured a master gunner, three sergeants, three corporals and forty men, together with some contribution money meant for the pay of the garrison. Strong parties of Roundhead troops were stationed at Odiham and Alton to curtail the garrison's raiding activities. On 7 May he cut off a party from the House who had gone out to collect some "contribution money" in the vicinity. Twelve horsemen, mostly officers, were taken. On 6 July 1644, "Tis true the rebels are most vengeful against Basing as appears by their usage of Captain Rosewell sometime apothecary in the Old Bailey who (because he belonged to the garrison of Basing) was clapped up in prison in Farnham Castle and there lodged in so noisome a hole (the rebels made it so) as it is not conceivable how a man could breath in it above two hours".[53] Yet these were just petty annoyances compared with what was to come.

We must follow for a little the progress of the two great Parliament armies as they march off our stage and into the wings. The King advanced to Reading and three days later retired to his headquarters at Oxford, having destroyed the defences at Reading and evacuated the town. Essex and Waller, no great admirers of each other, now joined in a sort of combined operations set up but never united their commands. On 14 May the Captain General Essex marched from Beaconsfield. His force consisted of at least eleven regiments of foot and seven of horse as well as a company of dragoons and a substantial train of artillery. Sir William Waller stayed at Farnham until Friday, 17 May and then marched out in the direction of Wallingford. His Force was 8 regiments of foot, 8 of horse, sixty wagons for baggage and ammunition and twenty four guns of various calibres. Both armies were destined for eventual disaster and near disaster.

---

[53] Mercius Aulicus

Chapter Six

'THE RING OF FIRE'

Be courageous and God will bless you,
Lie still and you perish.
A London Tract, July 1643.

WITH THE FIELD SERVICE taking Waller and Essex into the Midlands it might be anticipated that those in the House would have a period of quiet when the damage inflicted by Waller's rough handling might be repaired and life return to something approaching normality. But in fact nothing could be further from the truth. Colonel Richard Norton, known for some inexplicable reason to his friend Cromwell as "Idle Dick", having been personally affronted by his earlier repulse, took over where Waller left off and pressed the siege with vigour. To those who think of sieges in terms of a garrison penned immovably inside walls while the enemy prowl hungrily outside, it will come as a surprise to learn that the garrison of Basing were forever making raids from the House, sometimes for food, sometimes for money but always to confound and annoy the enemy and to keep him on the alert. On one occasion the Marquess and Colonel Rawdon, the Governor, called a Council of War and planned a raid on Odiham where there was always a Roundhead outpost on duty. Two local men were to guide the attackers "one with a dark lantern and the other with torches to fire the town". It was agreed that each man in the party should have five shillings before the march and that they should have all the plunder for the same. Obviously for success such an enterprise requires complete secrecy. Unfortunately for the Cavaliers they had a spy in the camp who forewarned their enemy, Colonel Samuel Jones, Governor of Farnham Castle.[54] A large proportion of the garrison, consisting of 80 horse and 200 foot, advanced stealthily through the night shrouded lanes, until about two o'clock in the morning they were detected by a sentry at Warnborough Mill "being about half a mile from Odiham", who challenged them and then sounded the alarm. Skirmishing then broke out with the Watch of Horse who were driven back. Soon the Cavaliers were to get a hotter reception than they expected for the Parliament troops from Farnham Castle were waiting for them. "Colonel Norton, in all this losing no time had by this got most part of his horse and drew them into the field, leaving the rest for the town and marching close to the enemy very furiously fell upon them with great valour, which caused the enemy presently to retreat.[55] So that when Colonel Jones fell on the front with his foot, the horse came in on the rear at which the enemy horse fled and all the foot were taken and the horse pursued almost to Basing House". A good haul of prisoners were taken as follows: Captain Rowland and his brother Lieutenant Rowland, Lieutenant Ivory, Ensign Coram, William Robinson, surgeon to the Marquess of Winchester, three Gentlemen at Arms, three sergeants, five drums and three drummers, seventy-five common soldiers, one quartermaster, five corporals and one sutler. Major Langley, described as "sometime a

---

[54] Siege Diary

[55] Norton's Victory etc. — full title in bibliography

mercer in Paternoster Row," was taken prisoner wounded "but was not recognised as he had been wily enough to disguise himself "in a poor habit more like a tinker than gentleman".[56] Thinking him of no consequence they let him go. Colonel Jones's report shows that this action took place close to the ruins of King John's Castle the shell of whose weathered keep still stands where the Whitewater River meets the Basingstoke Canal today. About four o'clock on the same day, Colonel Norton appeared before the House with three troops of horse and tried to draw the garrison out. But having lost a large proportion of his strength already, the Marquess was not to be tempted into any other rash venture, although we are told that Norton's trumpeters sounded a mocking call known as a "levett" several times, which must have sorely tried the temper of the fiery Cavaliers.

It was estimated after this disaster at Odiham that the garrison consisted of between 150 to 200 men. Once again the noose drew tight about the House as Parliamentary troops started to gather. Colonel Sir Richard Onslow commanded the Surrey forces. His redcoat regiment was five companies strong and his officers were Lieutenant Colonel Jordan (High Sheriff of Surrey), Major Hill (of Guildford), Captain Jordan (the High Sheriff's Son), Captain Cuffly, Captain Westbrook, Captain Perham, and Captain Warren. Colonel Richard Norton's Hampshire force consisted of one regiment of foot and one of horse, to which were added on 11 June three troops of horse. Colonel Herbert Morley brought six blue coated companies out of Sussex. Colonel Samuel Jones, Governor of Farnham Castle,

---

[56] Ibid

spared two companies of White Coats from his garrison. All this force, numbering about 2,000 men, "were drawn up before the House on the South of Basingstoke", that is to say, on the Park side.[57] At nightfall the army dispersed to its quarters: Onslow to Andwell House near to the ruins of the Priory, the White Coats to Sherfield, Morley's foot and Norton's horse were quartered in Basingstoke. And so for several days there were no more than small skirmishes as foraging parties from the House were met by Roundhead patrols. Short, sharp, and bloody as these chance encounters often were, it can be seen that there was not so far any planned offensive until Norton rejoined the force on 17 June.

Inside the House the depleted garrison was split into three watches so that they were ever vigilant. Two watches were always on duty while the other rested. Each captain and his company had a particular station which they would man when action threatened. The South face looking toward the Park was in the overall command of Major Cafaud, "the works in the Garden", that is to say about half of the North front, was in charge of Major Langley, whom we have already met at Odiham disguised in poor clothes.[58] Lieutenant Colonel Sir Robert Peake was entrusted with the disposition of the guns around the walls. A reserve was formed of Peake's musketeers to strengthen any part of the walls at need, while the very troopers of the House's horse were issued with muskets for the defence, very probably to their disgust. Even the senior officers had to keep watch and word, the only exception being Colonel Rawdon because of his great age. The Roundheads occupied the village, including the church "and

---

[57] Siege Diary

[58] Ibid

seized much cattle and corn, which the Marquess of Winchester ... had provided to be sent to him at the garrison of Basing House, but will now be better employed".[59] It would seem that Norton's intention in view of the failure of Waller's men to take the house by assault was to starve the garrison out, for he contented himself with throwing up breastworks on Cowdray's Down and in the Park. At this time the accounts are full of sallies from the House, small successes and failures, which no doubt provided a welcome relief from the boredom of siege warfare even if they achieved nothing else.

Towards the end of June, Colonel Norton again absented himself from Basing taking with him five troops of horse to join Sir William Waller's army.[60] About this time Basing House acquired another name among the merry Cavaliers to whom the stubborn resistance of the little garrison was a constant inspiration. It happened when a Cavalier newsheet commented that "Norton himself has gone to Sir William and left the work to others, thinking it ill manners to attempt that for which his general was so handsomely basted".[61] Before long the Cavaliers were drinking to "Basting House" and hereafter the treatment dealt out by the Marquess and his men to the besiegers was known as "basting".

Although out of the sphere of our narrative, the manoeverings of Essex and Waller's army have a bearing on the fortunes of Basing, so we must briefly recount them here. In the previous chapter we left those atmies en route to Oxford to trap the King. But events did not

---

[59] Moderate Intelligencer

[60] Young: Cropedy Bridge

[61] Mercurius Aulicus

turn out as intended. On 3 June the Royal Army slipped out of Oxford at night and marched north. On 6 June after a conference at Chipping Norton, Essex and Waller decided to part, the former to relieve the hard pressed garrisons of the West Country, the latter to shadow the King, a decision much criticised by historians and strategists ever since. It is sufficient to say that after following the King up and down the country, Waller thought he saw an opportunity to destroy his opponent and attacked across Cropredy Bridge near Banbury. Here he met with a severe check, sustaining 700 casualties whilst the Royalist losses were light. The King then proceeded to the West where eventually he trapped the Earl of Essex's army between himself and the forces of the Western Cavaliers and crushed it like an egg at Lostwithiel. Essex escaped by boat and the horse cut their way out but it was a disaster of the first magnitude. Waller fared little better for, as Clarendon remarks, "the defeat of that day at Cropredy was much greater than it then appeared to be and that it even broke the heart of his army".[62] By the time Waller reached Northampton on 3 July there was now no question of following the King, for he had lost half his army by desertion. On the 26 July, Waller returned to London leaving the remnants of his army at Abingdon.

Basing was left, as it were, in a vacuum. While it was true that it need not fear the return of either of the Parliament armies, the Royalist armies were far away, one in the North under Rupert, where it was resoundingly beaten by the Allied Armies at Marston Moor on 2 July, and the other, victorious in the West, as we have seen. For the time there was no chance of outside interference, hostile or friendly. Colonel Herbert Morley was now, in the absence of Norton, in

---

[62] Clarendon Book Eight

command of the besiegers, and he pushed the work of encirclement forward with grim determination. He repaired and extended the breastworks that Waller's men had originally made and erected new batteries: gradually trenches crept toward the House. Morley's pikemen and musketeers blanketed the South, or Park side, while Onslow's men were on the right of Morley's and covered the lower lane to Basingstoke and the close between, known to this day as Slaughter Close. Guards of horse continually patrolled the area between the Lane and the church which had been turned into a stable. The blue coats who were quartered there and in the surrounding village had broken open the tomb house of the Paulets and cast the leaden coffins into bullets. The result of this blockade soon made itself felt. Flour became short, there being no mill available to grind corn, presently even corn itself became scarce.[63] Salt and other necessities were exhausted. The hay in the meadows was denied to the Cavaliers' chargers, while the corn now going golden in the meadows around Pyotts or Magpie Hill would fall to the use of Parliament, not to the Marquess on whose land it was growing. This grim and constant squeeze by Morley was more to be feared than all of Waller's cannon, and belts were tightened in the House.

That the Parliament forces were not content to sit around forever is shown when "two mortar pieces were sent to Basing this day and divers granadoes which we hope will provide good instruments for gaining Basing House for we are certified that the besiegers have entrenched themselves firmly".[64] The mortar piece ranged from 12½ inches to 41 inches in calibre with the shell up to 80lbs in weight.

---

[63] Siege Diary

[64] Weekly Account

The method of firing these monsters was complex, slow, and required considerable nicety of judgement. After the propellent powder had been placed in the chamber of the mortar, a board cut to fit the bore of the piece was fitted in, covered with turf, then with earth.[65] Finally, on top of the earth the shell with its fuse was made to rest in such a manner that it was only partially enclosed in the bore. The gunner lighted the fuse of the shell with one hand and fired the piece with the other. This was called double firing and a tedious, dangerous business it seems to have been. But the effect of a well-placed mortar shell had devastating effect.

While these huge engines of war were making their slow passage to Basing the industrious Morley was directing the completion of a small fort in the park. To the experienced watchers on the wall it was obvious that such a labour was not to shield a light saker but a heavy cannon. They were not mistaken, for a culverin had been installed, a massive piece weighing almost two tons with a 5½ inch bore, firing an 18lb shot propelled by an 18lb charge, which soon opened fire, sending six of the heavy projectiles hurtling into the House. Colonel Onslow's men working like beavers on a platform in the lane, completed it in the space of 24 hours and installed another heavy cannon called a demi culverin which also opened fire. Although half the size of a culver in, it had a bore 4½ inches in diameter and threw a 9lb shot propelled by a 9lb charge. As time wore on the trenches and breastworks crept ever closer to the walls of "Loyalty House" and by the end of July were stated in the Marquess's Diary to be within "a half musket shot". With the enemy at such close quarters the garrison could no longer walk carelessly on the ramparts, several

---

[65] Godwin

being killed or wounded until they learned caution, even the Marquess being shot through the clothes, a narrow escape indeed.

Onslow's Surrey redcoats were reinforced at this time by a further four companies, while a company from Southampton, 140 strong, joined Colonel Morley, coming by way of Hackwood. No doubt thinking that it would be to his credit at this time if he could prevail on the Marquess to surrender before the return of Norton, Morley sent a drummer with the following demand. "My Lord — To avoid the effusion of Christian blood I have thought fit to send your lordship this summons to demand Basing House to be delivered to me for use of King and Parliament. If this be refused the ensuing inconvenience will rest upon you. I desire your speedy answer and rest, my Lord, Your humble servant, Herbert Morley".[66] He soon got his "speedy answer", sealed with a bullet. "Sir, It is a crooked demand and shall receive its answer suitable. I hold this House in the right of my Sovereign and will do it despite your Forces. Your letter I will preserve in the testimony of your rebellion. Winchester". Upon the return of the messenger the furious Morley opened up a cannonade which "beat down divers of our chimneys and made some breeches in the House".[67] The defenders had mounted some drakes (light field pieces) on the roofs from which eminence they had a good field of fire, which caused this casualty rate amongst the chimneys as the Parliament gunners sought to dislodge them. Shortage of salt was becoming critical in the House as was shown when rotten meat was thrown over the walls, there being no salt available to preserve it.

---

[66] Siege Diary

[67] Ibid

Before or about 22 July, Colonel Richard Norton returned from the Battle of Cropredy Bridge and resumed command of the operations. This same night, it being dark and stormy, the Marquess sent a messenger to Oxford with dispatches. This trooper, Edward Jeffrey, was a brave man for he had to make his way through the enemy lines and probably steal a horse to make his escape. Although he undoubtedly would be wearing the orange tawny scarf that originated with Essex, but was now the universal badge of Parliament, his ignorance of the password would soon lead to his apprehension, if challenged, while the bulky dispatches that lay like a heavy weight over his heart would automatically seal his death warrant if discovered. Such a man carried his life in his hands, yet we find that Jeffrey made the trip regularly. The bad weather which aided him also helped eight Roundhead prisoners, who slipped over the wall back to their comrades.

Hostilities continue with forays and sallies. The mortars having arrived we learn that in one night they fired six 36lb stone shot at the House. The Cavaliers formed a "blind" which was a loopholed structure of earth and timber from which snipers operated.[68] Next day Onslow's men had constructed one which enfiladed the approaches to it making it untenable. Toward the end of July a period of heavy rain flooded the trenches in the low lying ground at the foot of Cowdrays Down, forcing their evacuation. A culverin was set up by the church to endeavour to demolish a tower where snipers have become too persistent. These and other mundane activities made up the life of the soldiers who were engaged in the boring business of siege warfare. The garrison showed that they could still sting when,

---

[68] Ibid

on 28 July, a party of forty horse under Lieutenant Cuffaud of the garrison and Cornet Bryan of Peake's troop, made a surprise attack on the enemy's works, capturing a standard, killing twenty Roundheads, and "pursued the rebels to Basingstoke town end slashing and doing execution all the way".[69]

The Roundheads still continued with their siege works. Another cannon platform was raised on the east side in the "little wood" and connected to the church by a trench. In the early part of August nine more prisoners escaped. One wonders if they were allowed to do so to conserve rations. They reported that the garrison now consisted of 250 men, all weary of being penned up in the House. After the attack by Cafaud and Bryan, the guard on the works on Cowdrays Down was doubled and the men were issued with pikes to repel future cavalry attack. Morley's works in the Park had come near to completion. We see from Hollar's engraving how close the opposing breast works were, close enough we are told to throw hand grenades in. These were small iron shells about three inches in diameter filled with powder and equipped with a fuse. The first mention of their use was made in 1594. From the engraving also we see that the heavy culverin fire had not been ineffective, as a large tower on the outer walls is seen to be badly damaged and is labelled "the tower that is half battered down". But with a fighting spirit that seems never to have waned, and indeed to have flamed higher the greater the adversity, the Marquess sent out Major Cufaud with a body of musketeers and troopers to attack these breastworks in the Park and Lieutenant Snow with 30 men to attack the works in the lane. The latter was particularly successful, damaging the demi-culverin,

---

[69] Ibid

setting fire to the guard house and capturing a quantity of tools and ammunition. Cuffaud was hardly less successful, killing many of the besiegers, and actually bringing off a mortar and ammunition. Someone had to suffer for these daring raids, so Captain Orarn, the Roundhead Guard Commander, was court martialled, charged with negligence and cowardice, barely escaping with his life.

Hay for the garrison's horses was getting low so the Cavaliers constructed an earthwork in front of the grange to cover their men when they crept out under the cloak of darkness to cut sedge and grass for their mounts.[70] Toward nightfall on 14 August, the restless horsemen were out again under Lieutenant Cuffaud and Cornet Bryan who led forty musketeers as well as twenty horse. Their objective was once more the works on Cowdrays Down. Again the guard of horse was routed. But these wild riders had come that way once too often. The superior strength of the Roundheads overcame them, Bryan was overpowered and taken, three others wounded, and Ensign Amory killed.[71] On 19 August, a demi-cannon was fetched up to the platform in the wood. This was a really heavy weapon, 12ft in length and weighing almost 3 tons, throwing a 27lb shot. On this day it threw 48 of these missiles into the House. This seems to have been the signal for a general cannonade which continued during the next two days, about 160 shot, the smallest of which was 18lb, being poured into the dwelling and its fortifications. Yet another culverin was brought up and situated in Olivers Delve, a chalkpit, which as I have previously stated, was still in existence in Bartons Lane until recently. Thus Loyalty House was ringed about by some of the

---

[70] Ibid

[71] Bryan taken August 14 exchanged about October 2

heaviest artillery of the day. The power of the projectiles can be seen in many places, in the still standing north front and particularly in the west end of the Bloody Barn, and it seems incredible that the House was not reduced to a heap of rubble by the sheer weight of metal that assailed it. The biggest gun in the garrison was indeed broken and breaches appeared in a tower and a battery which officers and men laying aside their weapons and picking up spades, speedily repaired. The Marquess remarks in his Diary at this time: "Our necessities grow fast upon us, now drinking water and for some weeks making our bread with pease and oats, our stock of wheat being spent".

The earthworks which Parliament had constructed now extended completely round the House, being over a mile in circumference. More heavy guns were on their way from Portsmouth. Colonel Richard Norton, thinking that any man's spirit must now be broken by the combination of heavy bombardment and half rations, on Monday, 4 September sent another summons to the House. "My Lord — These are in the name and by the authority of the Parliament of England the highest Court of Justice in this kingdom to demand the House and Garrison of Basing to be delivered to me, to be disposed of according to act of Parliament. And hereof I expect your answer by this Drum within one hour of the receipt hereof. In the meantime I rest. Yours to serve you — Richard Norton. From the quarters before Basing the 2 of September in the afternoon."[72] But if he expected any sign of weakening from John Paulet he had underestimated the man. Back came the inflexible reply: "Sir — Whereas you demand the House and Garrison of Basing by a pretended authority of Parliament, I answer that without the King

---

[72] Siege

there can be no Parliament, but by his Majesty's Commission I keep this place and without his absolute command shall not deliver it to any pretenders whatsoever. I am, yours to serve you. Winchester". Being refused once again, Norton commanded the battery in the wood to open fire. Within six hours that battery fired 120 rounds of shot into the House generally and particularly into the great brick corner turret, which crumbled and collapsed, killing three men who presumably were manning it. Godwin states that when he was at the ruins about 1880, the remains of these towers were still plainly visible on the slope above the canal. To avoid this breach being stormed and to prevent that end of the South front being enfiladed, it had to be built up again with baulks of timber, debris and earth to a great thickness. This small wood mentioned by the Marquess in his diary description of the House and referred to so often in our narrative was, to my mind, situated in the angle at the cross roads where modern Crown Lane and Milking Pen Lane meet, where even today quite a stand of timber still exists.

The Marquess then sent a last desperate message to Cavalier headquarters at Oxford, stating that he could hold out another ten days "then must I submit to the worst conditions the rebels are like to grant to my person and religion".[73]

Several times a Council of War had been held at Oxford to consider how best they might relieve Basing, at the urgent requests of the Marchioness who had come to the Cavalier headquarters to solicit help for her husband. Being a lady of considerable influence related both to the Earl of Essex and to the Marchioness of Hertford, her requests could not easily be ignored. While her religion

---

[73] Clarendon Vol. 3.

predisposed the numerous Roman Catholics in the town toward her cause and induced them to offer themselves and then- servants in the service. But the Governor, Sir Arthur Aston, took the commonsense view that there was forty miles of enemy held territory between themselves and the Marquess. There were Roundhead garrisons at Abingdon, at Reading and at Newbury, whose patrols left no yard of highway unguarded. Clarendon states:[74] "The Governor opposed the design as full of more dangers and liable to more dangers than any soldier who understood command would expose himself and the King's Service to and protested that he would not suffer any of the small garrison that was under his charge to be hazarded in the attempt". And the Governor's cautious Council carried the day until the receipt of the Marquess's desperate message. At once another Council was held. Colonel Henry Gage, the 17th century epitome of Chaucer's "perfect gentle knight", in the face of the Governor's reiterated refusal, proposed a compromise and declared "That though he thought the service full of hazard especially the return, yet if the Lords would, by enlisting their own servants, persuade the gentlemen in the town to do the like and engage their own persons whereby a good troop or two might be raised (upon whom the principal dependance must be) and would willingly, if there were no one else thought fitter, undertake the conduct of them himself, and he hoped he would give a good account of it".[75] We are told that the Governor purely hated Gage on account of his remarkable achievements both as a soldier and a man, and for the way that everyone deferred to him

---

[74] Ibid

[75] Ibid

in the Councils of War.[76] We can believe that this suggestion did not endear Gage further to the Governor. "The Lords mounted their servants upon their own horses and they with the volunteers who frankly enlisted themselves amounted to a body of 250 very good horse all put under the command of Colonel William Webb, an excellent officer".[77] Greenland House near Henley upon Thames had fallen to Parliament after a heroic defence. The troops were allowed to march out with the honours of war (i.e. with their arms, colours flying and drums beating) and Colonel Hawkin's Regiment of 300 men had arrived at Oxford from thence and had subsequently recruited another 100 men who also were to go. Sir William Campion, Governor of Boarstall House, ventured at this time to add his horse to the relief force. Twelve barrels of powder and 1,200 lb of match were to be taken.

At the head of this stalwart band, Gage marched out of Oxford at about 10 o'clock on the night of 9 September. The old ruse of pretending to be a Parliamentary force was employed, the officers wearing orange sashes and the men having orange ribbons in their hats. They marched steadily all that night, very well aware of the urgency of their mission. At dawn near Wallingford they were further strengthened by a band of 50 cavalry and 50 musketeers of the Wallingford garrison under Captain Walters and the tired men were rested three hours. Gage sent off a messenger to Sir William Ogle, Governor of Winchester Castle, who had previously pledged a body of 100 horse and 300 foot for the relief whenever they should be required, requesting that they should be prepared to attack the

---

[76] Ibid

[77] Ibid

rebels' quarters on the Park side of the House between 4 and 5 o'clock in the morning of 11 September. Gage was to attack by way of the Grange, while the Marquess was to sally out from the House. By this three pronged attack it was hoped to cause enough confusion in the Parliament ranks to get through to the House. Having rested his men, "he marched forward with as much speed as the foot soldiers could manage until he came by bye lanes to the village of Aldermaston".[78] He sent on ahead Captain Walters with his troop and the quartermaster of each regiment to obtain refreshment for the men on their arrival, intending to have another two hours' rest period. But Walters, finding a patrol of Parliament soldiers at Aldermaston, and forgetting both the need for secrecy and the fact that they were masquerading as Roundheads, fired on them killing one and capturing six. What Gage said to the impetuous Walters can only be guessed, but in any case recriminations were superfluous for in no time the news reached Norton that the relief force was close at hand. Approaching the village the foot were lagging badly which was hardly surprising for they had scarcely had three hours rest since leaving Oxford. To ease them as much as possible, Gage dismounted and ordered all the horse to do likewise and caused the foot soldiers to mount.[79] After three miles of slow progress they reached Aldermaston about eight o'clock in the evening. By eleven they were on the move again and marched all night, the horsemen again taking the foot up behind them to rest from time to time. In the early morning of Wednesday 11 September, Gage's force arrived at Chineham Down, two miles from the House. It was a morning of

---

[78] Ibid

[79] Life of Gage

thick fog which shrouded their objective and its surroundings from view. Having been informed of the approach of the relief force the Marquess commanded fires to be lit on top of the great gate house as a sign of readiness.[80] But here a serious setback to Gage's plans awaited him. Lieutenant Swainley of the Winchester garrison awaited him with a dispatch from Ogle. The expected help upon which he so depended was not coming. Major Ludlow and his Parliamentary horse were between Winchester and Basing and Ogle "durst not send troops".[81] Robbed of both his support and the element of surprise Gage abandoned his original plan and holding a council of war decided to attack at one spot hoping to drive a wedge through the enemy lines. Instructing the men to tie a white handkerchief above the right elbow so that they should be recognisable to the Basing garrison, encouraging them with promises of pay and loot he prepared for the supreme effort. Colonel Webb led the right wing and Lieutenant Colonel Boncle the left wing of the horse and Colonel Gage himself the foot. Gage's report reads: "Upon a little rising or ascent near certain hedges lined with the enemy's musketeers, we discovered a body of five troops of horse standing in very good order to receive us. But before we could come up to them we were saluted from the hedges with a smart volley of musket shot, more terrible (frightening) than damageable, for Colonel Webb with the right wing of the horse charged at them so gallantly that in a moment they turned head and ran away". Clarendon says: "After a shorter resistance than was expected from the known courage of Norton, though many men fell, the enemy horse gave ground and at last plainly ran to a safe

---

[80] Siege Diary

[81] Life of Gage

place". Mercurius Aulicus relates: "The rebel foot fought better, more especially Colonel Morley's Regiment", but the Royalist musketeers drove them back yard by yard until they too retreated, the fog covering their withdrawal Gage continued to advance, sounding his trumpets and drums to let those in the House know of his close proximity.

The Marquess decided that the time had come for him to take a hand in the game. A body of musketeers commanded by Lieutenant Colonel Johnson sallied forth from the grange and attacked the Parliament breastworks on Cowdray's Down. Taken front and rear, the Roundheads scattered like chaff before the wind, thus opening a passage into the House into which Gage brought his men and his powder.[82] It needs little imagination to conjure up the scenes of relief and joy after so much privation and hardship as the Oxford force marched in through the garrison gateway, the arch of which still stands. But Gage was not a man to waste time in self congratulation while there was work still to be done. Having "paid my Lord Marquess the respects due to a person of his merit and quality", and having assigned 100 musketeers of Colonel Hawkins's Regiment to join the garrison, the Royalist Cavalry and Foot again broke out of the House and, under the fire of the Parliament artillery, gained Chineham Down once more.[83] Leaving a patrol to observe the enemy's movements they proceeded into Basingstoke where then as now Wednesday was market day. The Parliament Committee that had lodged in the town soon vanished at his approach and Gage was opposed only by the black scowls of the townsfolk as he rode in.

---

[82] Siege Diary

[83] Gage's Report

Well might they scowl, for he commandeered, "100 cattle whereof divers were excellent fat oxen, as many or more sheep and 40 and odd hogs".[84] Gage's report further amplifies the matter: "From thence (Basingstoke) I continued to send all day as much wheat, malt, salt, oats, bacon, cheese and butter as I could get carts and horses to transport", as well as a little magazine of 13 barrels of powder.[85]

In the meantime Major Cafaude with a hundred musketeers and Captain Hull with a similar number of the Oxford force, had struck hard against the enemy in Basing village, recapturing the church which had been fortified, taking prisoner Captains Jarvas (Jervoise?) and John Jephson. "both heirs to great fortunes", as well as a lieutenant, two sergeants and about 30 soldiers.[86] The rest escaped into the strong fort erected in the Park. Meanwhile Lieutenant-Colonel Robert Peake had led another party against Sir Richard Onslow's quarters near the Basingstoke Bulwark in the meadow now known as Slaughter Close. There they met with equal success, destroying the sconces, capturing a piece of artillery and setting fire to the enemy's tents and huts. Thus the garrison remained in possession of the approach to the House during the critical period when the victual trains approached from Basingstoke. Having put enough provisions into the House to last two months, Colonel Gage then began to contemplate how to withdraw to Oxford, a problem which might have perplexed an Alexander.

---

[84] Clarendon

[85] Gage's Report

[86] Siege Diary. Jervois exchanged October 2

The enemy were gathered all along his line of retreat in strength. 500 horse and dragoons were at Aldermaston under Major General Browne; a detachment from Newbury 300 strong was at Thatcham; the garrison from Reading at Padworth guarding all the routes of access over the Rennet.[87] As soon as Norton perceived that he was out of the House and beyond aid, no doubt he would be prepared to fall on Gage's rear as well as sending messengers ahead to warn the other forces. It was a difficult decision fraught with disaster, but Gage solved it in a masterly way. He withdrew under cover of darkness and fog on Thursday night 12 September, "without sound of drum or trumpet", and again assuming Parliamentary disguise, "giving ourselves out to be Parliament troops marching from before Basing House to the River Kennet to lie in wait for the Oxford troops.[88] Guided by two scouts who knew the locality he found a way to cross the Kennet at Burghfield, the bridge having been destroyed by the enemy, the troopers swimming their horses across with a footsoldier mounted behind them. Knowing that both Reading and Henley bridges were down Gage crossed the Thames in the same manner at Pangbourne and so reached Wallingford in safety at 8 o'clock Friday morning arriving back in Oxford the next day, 14 September.[89] Thus was the ability of Basing House to resist restored, an exploit that earned Colonel Henry Gage a well deserved knighthood in an age when that honour was not so lightly bestowed as at present.

---

[87] Godwin

[88] Gage's Report

[89] Life of Gage

With the relief force gone, it was not long before the ring of fire closed its vice-like grip on the House once more. 100 musketeers under Captain Fletcher were holding the newly gained village and church and celebrating their good fortune, were carousing. A sudden attack, led by Colonel Norton in person, took Fletcher's men by surprise and they started to give way. But reinforcements from the House arrived and after a short sharp fight the besiegers were driven off. It was at this time that a great calamity befell the garrison for Lieutenant Colonel Thomas Johnson was shot in the shoulder and died a fortnight later. Clarendon speaks highly of him and states: "he was no less eminent in the garrison for his valour and conduct as a soldier than famous throughout the kingdom for his excellency as a herbalist and physician".

But Norton was not long to be held at bay. By 23 September he had retaken the church and once again closed the approaches to the House.[90] The month of October was a month of skirmishes with small triumphs and disasters for the garrison. But things were coming to a head on the national stage. On the 15th, King Charles reached Salisbury, fresh from his victory over Essex at Lostwithiel. Meanwhile, incredibly Essex had been entrusted with another army, and three Parliament armies met at Basingstoke on 22 October. These were the Earl of Manchester's Army of the Eastern Association whose horse contained the famous double regiment of Ironsides under Lieutenant General Oliver Cromwell, Sir William Waller's and the Earl of Essex's. Joined to these were Sir James Harrington's brigade of the London Trained Bands numbering about 3,000 men. The artillery train numbered 24 pieces and the total

---

[90] Siege Diary

strength of the combined armies were 1,000 foot and 8,000 horse.[91] The lofty watch towers of Basing made an admirable grandstand for observing all this considerable activity. The Marquess's Diary notes that the vanguard of the Army was stationed at Rooks Down (where Park Prewett Hospital now stands), the main body at Basingstoke, and the rear at Hackwood. The Marquess must have felt uncomfortable with these neighbours even though he knew their purpose was to fight the King. Had they turned their attention to him in such strength he must have been crushed like an egg under a hammer.

By 25 October two of the King's objectives had been realized. Donnington Castle near Newbury had been besieged for over a month and was relieved on 18 October. On 21 October its Commander, Colonel John Boys, was knighted by the King. Banbury Castle had been beset for three months. On 25 October Charles detached the Earl of Northampton with his brigade of cavalry to the assistance of the 18 year old commander at Banbury, William Compton — the Earl's brother. Twice the enemy had stormed the walls and twice been repulsed, provisions were so low that all but two of the horses had been eaten. The relief was only just in time. Compton too was knighted. Basing's turn had to wait.

Despite a disparity of two to one in favour of Parliament, the King took up a defensive position. As the three armies approached, on paper he should have been obliterated. But Charles drew up his main body at Speen Heath where it was partially protected by the guns of Donnington Castle. He also left a strong detachment at Shaw House northeast of Newbury. Wedgewood is of the opinion that Charles

---

[91] Young: Hastings to Culloden

meant to wait for reinforcements under Prince Rupert to come up.[92] Waller and Manchester decided to force the King to fight before Rupert's arrival. Essex, Waller, and Cromwell were to march to the North and attack Speen Heath from the West, while Manchester was to attack Shaw House. Caught between two fires the King was bound to get burnt, or so it was reasoned. But the two attacks were uncoordinated and the fighting as at Newbury was inconclusive. The Royalist line held everywhere. The King withdrew into Donnington Castle where he held a council of war. Having drawn all his cannon into the Castle, he went to join Rupert, taking Charles, Prince of Wales with him. The Royal Army began to fall back on Oxford and so demoralised were the Parliamentarians that they made no effort to stop them. They had little to congratulate themselves upon. Charles had evaded them and despite the two-to-one odds had severely mauled them.

Reinforced by Rupert, and with his numbers more even now at 15,000, the Royalists advanced boldly on Donnington on 9 November with all due ceremony "beating drums, colours flying and trumpets prattling", but except for a half hearted attempt to stop them with musketeers, Parliament allowed them to retrieve the precious cannon from Donnington and fall back on Lambourne without further effort.[93]

The events following the achievement of the King's final objective before moving into winter quarters is best told by Clarendon. "His (the King's) heart was set upon the relief of Basing, which was now again distressed". This was indeed true as at this time the officers

---

[92] Wedgewood: King's War, p. 379.

[93] Young: Hastings to Culloden

were on a ration of one meal a day, the soldiers being given two. The beer had all been consumed, everyone was drinking water which no doubt the men found less endurable than short rations. "He had a great mind to do so with his whole army that thereby he might draw the enemy to battle; but on full debate it was concluded that the safest way would be to do it by a strong party, that 1,000 horse should be drawn out, everyone of which should carry before him a bag of corn or other provision and march so as to be at Basing House the following morning after they parted from the army, and then every trooper should cast his bag down to make their retreat as best they might. Colonel Gage who had such good success before was appointed to command this party which he cheerfully undertook to do".[94] But as it turned out there was no need to cut their way through. For the day before Gage arrived the enemy raised the siege of their own accord. It would seem that their reasons could well have been threefold. The King's army, which had fought the three Parliament armies to a standstill at Second Newbury, might well advance to the relief of Basing. With their numbers reduced to 700 from 2,000 by desertion, disease, and casualties, they were in no position to give battle against such a strength as the King mustered, and in any case winter was approaching fast. They had blockaded the House for 24 weeks and had used a vast quantity of gunpowder. So at 8 o'clock in the morning of 19 November, laden waggons were seen to be leaving the Parliament position in the direction of Odiham, followed at midday after firing their hutted encampment.[95] A few troops of horse were left to cover their rear. Once more the stout walls of Loyalty

---

[94] Clarendon

[95] Siege Diary

House and the stouter hearts within had withstood the worst the enemy could do. The next evening, Gage's force of 1,000 horse brought in a welcome supply of ammunition and food. They found the garrison down to the barest of necessities, the soldiers spent and threadbare.[96] Besides the wounded and deserters they had lost a hundred men through the action and sickness. Plainly they had been at breaking point. Staying there three days they amply victualled the garrison. Not perhaps without reason John Paulet, Marquess of Winchester, attributes the deliverance to divine providence. "Let no man speak himself an instrument only giving thanks that God made him so. He chose the weak to confound the strong. Not unto us, O Lord, but to thine own name be all glory for ever. Amen." So runs the final entry in the Siege Diary.

---

[96] Ibid

Chapter Seven

'DISASTER'

Let who can have the day with your favour,
Both Armies are losers for their labours,
Much precious blood is lost, many a poor
soul

Stephen Buckley, 1643.

AFTER A QUIET WINTER during which much needed repairs were carried out, provisions and ammunition were restocked and everything made ready for the new campaigning season of 1645, which the Marquess had good reason to believe would include a further visitation from Parliament under one commander or another. All went smoothly until the garrison was split asunder by religious differences.

Apparently some jealousy arose over the fact that the military governor of Easing, Sir Marmaduke Rawdon (whom we have seen conducting himself with so much valour), was of the Protestant faith while a large number of the garrison were Roman Catholics. One is surprised that the Marquess himself took part in this dispute when up to that time he had shown so much sagacity. How foolish to risk the safety of the House with religious bigotry! But most men have an Achilles heel and this apparently was his. So we find him presenting a petition to the Privy Council in these terms.[97] "To the Right Honourable the Lords of his Majesty's Privy Council. The humble petition of his Majesty's Catholic Subjects of the Garrison of Basing House. Sheweth that your petitioners both during the time of the siege, which for some months continued against this place and since the raising thereof had just cause to suspect divers persons of this Garrison, for by reason of their different opinions from us we do generally hold it more safe that this garrison which has been very serviceable to his Majesty may consist of persons (both officers and men) of one religion. Therefore to prevent such inconveniences as may arise the petitioners humbly pray that the premises may be taken in to consideration to the end that it may be declared whether it may not be requisite that your petitioners who are most deeply engaged in this present war, may not be thought the fairest defendants and maintainers of a place of that strength and concernment. And your petitioners shall pray etc. Winchester." That the Privy Council would grant his request was, of course, a foregone conclusion and Basing was duly declared a Catholic garrison. Colonel Rawdon was asked to leave with all his men. And on 1st May, 1645 he did so, taking with him 500 horse and foot This was a monumental folly, the major factor leading to the eventual destruction of the House. Rawdon was ordered to join Goring's army, which, after some adventures he did.

Had the Marquess known it, he was under discussion "by the[98] gentlemen of Hants and Sussex". They examined the two previous sieges and at some length decided that instead of a blockade or a frontal assault, both of which had proved costly and ineffective, it

---

[97] Godwin

[98] Mercurius Rusticus

would be as well to employ a skilled engineer to apply a scientific approach to the problem. But while these weighty matters were under consideration things were moving to a head nationally. Cromwell had formed his New Model Army, a body not under the independent command of generals who oftimes hated one another and refused to co-operate, but under the single command of a General in Chief, the Yorkshire knight, Sir Thomas Fairfax. The King was eager for a battle that would decide the issue once and for all. Destroy the New Model and England was as good as his. This battle took place at Naseby on 14 June 1645 and ended in the total destruction of the King's "Oxford Army". Charles lost his infantry, all his guns, and most of his baggage. His personal and private papers were captured, the plunder was reckoned to be of the order of one hundred thousand pounds in gold, silver, and jewels.[99] With the defeat of Lord George Goring and his "Western Army" at Langport on 10 July, the collapse of the King's cause was total and complete. Now all that remained was to reduce the fortified towns, manor houses, and other strongholds that still held out for Charles.

The "Cunning Engineer" who was sent to Basing was one Colonel John Dalbier, a Dutchman with a fine record of service in the Parliament cause, having risen from the command of a troop of Lord Bedford's horse at the outbreak of war to the senior command of the besieging force. On 19 August Parliament issued 400 bandoliers, 400 swords, 300 muskets, 200 pieces and 10 drums to the Portsmouth garrison troops to be employed in the service at Basing. Dalbier reached Basing the following day with a force of 800 horse and foot. The garrison were mightily surprised that they committed no hostile

---

[99] Wedgewood

act, so they sent out a party of skirmishers and took prisoner an officer and nine troopers. On 23 August Captain Blagrave's company from Reading arrived, then later a further 100 musketeers from Southwark joined them. Mercurious Aulicus, made great fun of all this inactivity. "The engineer fell to his pretence, the work itself is money", it chortles on 20 August.[100] But it seems that Dalbier was laying his plans slowly and methodically, looking at the structures before him with an engineer's eye, considering how much leverage should be applied, and whereto, to bring about a dramatic collapse of the whole structure under consideration with the least expenditure of material. A month later he had sited his batteries and opened fire. A great tower in the old House or Castle collapsed on 22 September; then the guns were turned on the New House. It was an example of scientific fire having a great effect than the random fire of Norton's siege. First bricks were loosened in the main fabric then a long sinuous crack appeared in the wall, then the cannons were turned against the huge corner turret which came crashing to the ground, bringing with it a great slab of the wall so that rooms were exposed and "our men saw beds and bedding and other goods fall into the court".[101] By this time Dalbier had 1,000 foot and four troops of horse which were not sufficient to envelope the House completely as Norton and Morley had done. About this date too, we read of the use of a kind of poison gas, surely the first time it was used? Wet straw impregnated with brimstone and arsenic was set afire and the noxious fumes carried into the House by the wind.[102] Whether this was

---

[100] Mercurius Aulicus August 20

[101] Weekly Account October 1st

[102] Mercurius Verdicus No. 23

poisonous or just a nuisance is not known, but the Parliament papers commented on it with smug satisfaction, the Royalist papers as usual with mocking sarcasm.

Leaving Basing for the moment let us see the fate of Winchester whose fortunes we have followed as a major piece in the jigsaw of the Great Civil War locally. Late in September, Lieutenant General Oliver Cromwell was intent on reducing such places that still stood for the King and on making safe the passage of traders along the main roads. He had with him his own regiment, Colonel Charles Fleetwood's Regiment, Colonel John Pickering's Regiment and Colonel Hardress Waller's Regiment (foot). A formidable force indeed! Arriving before the gates of Winchester, he sent a summons to the Mayor, William Longland, couched in these terms. "Sir, I come not to this city but with a full resolution to save it and the inhabitants from ruin. I have commanded the soldiers upon pain of death that no wrong be done which I shall strictly observe. Only I shall expect you to give me access into the City without necessitating me to force my way, which if I do then it will not be in my power to save you or it. I expect your answer in half an hour. Your servant, Oliver Cromwell".[103] To which the mayor returned a conciliatory reply to the effect that the city was not his to render up but the governor, Sir William Ogle's, that he would try to make Ogle see sense, but that was all he could do. But replies such as this only raised Cromwell's ire and without more ado he forced his way into the city.

The garrison shut themselves up in the castle, the site of which is now largely covered by the Green Jackets' barracks and houses. It was on the West face of the city walls, and was originally fortified

---

[103] Godwin

by William the Conqueror. We are fortunate, indeed, that the County Hall still survives in which so much English History was made throughout the ages. The famous table of King Arthur, which is displayed high on the West wall, bears the work of Henry VIII's Sergeant Painter but was accounted of great antiquity even then. According to Milner it is riddled with musket balls fired by the soldiers of Parliament.[104] Cromwell pounded away at the castle with his great guns, demolishing towers and opening great breaches in the walls until on 8 October Ogle requested to know the terms of surrender. Although his defence of the castle seems to, have been a little half-hearted considering the strength of the place, it may have seemed pointless to continue the struggle in view of the King's total defeat in the field. After an all night discussion it was agreed that the castle and all it's contents should be rendered up and that Lord Ogle and his officers should retain their arms and Ogle his colours.[105] He should march out with. 100 armed men of his guard and be given safe conduct. All the rest of the garrison should be disarmed and dispersed. Cromwell reported to his commander-in-chief, Sir Thomas Fairfax: "... The works were exceeding good and strong. It's very likely that it would have cost much blood to take by storm. We have not lost 12 men."

Using the captured gun-powder totally to destroy the defences, Oliver then looked toward Basing.[106] On Tuesday, 7 October he marched, and camped that night at Alresford where his great friend Richard Norton resided at the manor house. Continuing his march

---

[104] Milner Book 2 P. 165

[105] Cromwells Report

[106] Milner

next morning, he arrived at Basingstoke and drew up his men in the field between Hackwood and the town, which can only mean, of course, on the present Basingstoke Common. Some were dispatched to the familiar encampment in the Park. Dalbier was said to be "on the other side where he had placed his batteries close to Basing Town", or, to be more precise, in Norton's old position on Cowdrays Down.[107] "The great gum which Lieutenant-General Cromwell brought with him were drawn up on the South-East side of the House", that is to say, on the Park side toward the village, possibly in that little wood we have heard so much of before.[108] The Moderate Intelligencer informs us that these "great guns" were heavy metal indeed.[109] One was the heaviest type of cannon then employed a "cannon royal", with a bore of 8 inches, a weight of 8,000 lbs, and firing a shot weighing 63 lbs, while two others were demi cannon weighing 6,000 lbs, twelve feet long, and throwing a 27lb shot. The forces surrounding the House numbered 7,000 men while the garrison, severely weakened by the loss of Rawdon's Regiment, numbered about 300. It was later estimated, that the defences really required a force of 800 men adequately to man them.[110] As soon as Cromwell arrived in person he and Colonel Dalbier carried out a reconnaissance of the House with the latter probably pointing out the targets and angles of fire he had planned. If they would not surrender then Dalbier intended to reduce the place to so many heaps of indefensible rubble. In three days Cromwell's guns were planted in

---

[107] Scottish Dove No. 104

[108] Mercurius Veridicus October 11th

[109] Moderate Intelligencer

[110] Cromwells Report

new redoubts and were ready for action.[111] Before Cromwell began operations he sent a final surrender demand to the Marquess, telling him that they (the garrison) had been evil neighbours, using the country people hardly.[112] They were a nest of Romanists and so of all others could worst make their arms good against Parliament and therefore must look for no mercy if they stood out to the utmost period but all the severity in a just way of arms might be made good. This still met with a flinty refusal. One wonders why the Marquess still held on, with his House gradually being beaten into pieces round his ears. Was it just a blind dogged refusal to accept defeat, or was he afraid that the garrison of professed Roman Catholics would be massacred by the relentless sectarians of the Parliament Army? We shall never know his reasons; perhaps it is only necessary to know the result of his refusal.

On Sunday 12 October, 1645, the guns began firing.[113] The next day being a dark and misty one, a party of horse stole out from the House, whether to try to escape or to have one last skirmish is not clear, but they surprised and captured two high officers, Colonel Hammond and Major King, who were riding out to visit Cromwell on the other side of the House.[114] Proposals to exchange them were immediately made to the Marquess, who refused. General Cromwell wrote back a blunt ultimatum. "If any wrong or harm is offered to these officers, the best in the House should not obtain quarter". Or in other words the Marquess own life would be forfeit if Hammond or

---

[111] Moderate Intelligencer October 13

[112] Ibid

[113] Scottish Dove No. 104

[114] Ibid

King died. All that day the guns thundered out ceaselessly and by nightfall the walls had at last been breached in two places large enough to permit storming parties to pass through.[115] Having many other matters that commanded his attention, Cromwell decided to make a swift end to the business of Basing House. His headquarters were in Basingstoke's London Street, at a place later to be called "Fleur de Lys" tavern, where Curry's shop stands at the present time. With the following day fixed for the assault, he spent much of the night in prayer. The subject which he chose for his meditations was the 115th Psalm.[116] "Not unto us, O God, not unto us, but unto thy name, give glory for thy mercy and truth's sake".

It was five o'clock on the morning of Tuesday 14 October, a thin mist rose from the Loddon marshes, the air was crisp and cold. In the Park and in the village the men of Parliament were standing to for the final effort. The plan of attack had been made the day before. It was to be an assault in strength. Colonel Dalbier and his men were to attack on the North side by the side of the Grange, next to him on his left hand Colonel John Pickering with his bluecoats.[117] Next was Hartop's Regiment, then the black coated regiment of Sir Hardress Waller. Colonel Montagu's Regiment of blues were on the extreme right. The men would be stamping and blowing on their hands to keep warm. Just as the clock struck six o'clock, four cannon crashed out.[118] It was the signal to attack. We can imagine Colonel Pickering, little in stature but great at heart, drawing his sword with a rasp of

---

[115] Ibid

[116] Peters

[117] Cromwells Report

[118] Ibid

steel. "Forward, my lads, in the name of God and the Parliament". All was silent, the only noise being the sound of their feet and the rattle of their accoutrements as they advanced. They were half way across the open expanse of the Park before they were seen. The alarm drums sounded their urgent call. There was the cry of "To arms, to arms, they are upon us!" The guard turned out and the Royalist soldiers, who had slept for the two years with one eye open and their weapons beside them were at their posts almost before they realised it. One moment the breaches were dark and empty, next day they were filled with the desperate men of the garrison prepared to sell their lives dearly.[119] Now the need for silence was over; a great shout went up from seven thousand throats "For God and Parliament"; like a giant wave they lapped up against the breeches on both sides of the House. Swords gleamed as they rose and fell, muskets blazed once, then were clubbed, smashing down on helmets until they broke and were cast aside. The air was full of tumult, with the screams of the wounded, moans of the dying, crack of pistols, savage war cries, and the rattling of drums. There was no holding that living tide and soon the breaches were carried and the Roundheads were inside those walls that had withstood them for so long.

The garrison fell back on the two Houses. The attackers stormed the New House sliding in at the windows. From the upper storeys the garrison showered down hand grenades. This continued resistance inflamed the wrath of the Roundhead soldiers and with cries of "Down with the Papists!" they sought them out and put them to the sword. They had by now also taken the bailey or courtyard in front of the Old House. There, the Royalist survivors continued with the

---

[119] True Informer No. 26

desperate resistance, firing the bridge which gave access from the courtyard into the great four storied gate house; showering hand grenades all the while. Colonel Pickering at the head of his men stormed and took the gateway, shouting "Fall on, fall on, all is ours!"[120] Colonels Montagus and Hardress Waller's men stormed a part of the wall where there was no breach, and beating back a Royalist party in a strong point there, drew up their scaling ladders and, using them to climb the moat and walls of the Old House, flooded over the parapet, Sir Hardress Waller being shot in the arm.[121] The garrison fought it out to the last, disputing every pass with the edge of the sword with desperate valour. This deepened the Parliament soldiers' rage and the cry arose again "Down with the Papists!", and many who had wished to surrender, having done all that brave men could, were butchered in cold blood. Major Robinson, in civilian life a comedian in the theatre at Drury Lane, was one of these. He attempted to surrender to Major Thomas Harrison, a fanatical Puritan, who shot him dead, exclaiming "Cursed be he that doeth the Lord's work negligently!" Several of the garrison, taking advantage of the confusion and seeing that they were unlikely to get quarter, slipped over the walls and made a break for it towards Hackwood. Some succeeded, some did not. One of the unfortunate ones was Major Caffaud, of whom we have heard so much. The fanatical Harrison, obviously more concerned with the death of the Catholics than with spoil, shot him from the ramparts.[122]

---

[120] Mercurius Civicus

[121] Cromwells Report

[122] Mercurius Civicus

Everywhere now was heard the splintering of doors as the Roundhead soldiers turned from battle to plunder. The Marquess of Winchester, having done all that a man could, even to ruining himself, surrendered to the captive Parliamentarian Colonel Hammond who stood by him, but even this did not prevent him losing his fine clothes to the angry soldiers. Sir Robert Peake bought his life by rendering up the key to his room, "exclaiming that they'd find enough treasure there", as indeed there was, there being £300 in a bag, a box of jewels, rings and bracelets, and a "box of curiously graven brass plates".[123] These latter were, of course, engraving plates, for Peake, in common with his fellow prisoners Hollar and Faithorne, was an engraver by trade. The ladies in the House were treated roughly but lost little more than their dignity as Hugh Peters, Cromwell's army chaplain, tells us:[124] "Eight or nine gentlewomen of rank, running together were entertained by the common soldiers somewhat coarsely, yet not uncivilly considering the action in hand … They left them with some clothes on them!" Some of the ladies were wounded in the last stages of the fighting when they tried to protect friends from the soldiers but only one was killed. This was the daughter of the Reverend Dr. Griffith, the Rector of the Church of St. Mary Magdalene in London, who had been taken prisoner and was gravely wounded. With more courage than good sense, much upset at the condition of her father, she started to "rail at our soldiers, calling them Roundheads and traitors".[125] An ill advised thing to provoke men still with the blood lust upon them, it was not surprising

---

[123] Ibid

[124] Peters Report

[125] Peters Report and Moderate Intelligencer

that presently "one of our soldiers cut her on the head and slew her, leaving her corpse shamefully naked". The wives of the Parliament soldiers must have welcomed them with open arms that night for amongst the spoil were one hundred rich dresses and petticoats the Mke of which they could never have afforded in a lifetime.[126] Meanwhile, Cromwell was assessing the purely military value of the House's contents.[127] The list runs: 11 cannon of various calibres, 20 barrels of powder with match proportionate, and a goodly store of bullets. 600 firearms, 100 pikes, 100 halberds, nine colours and 500 bandoliers. Hugh Peters says that all the rooms in both Houses, were completely furnished, provisioned for some years rather than months. As to the soldiers' plunder, it was beyond their wildest expectations. "The wealth of Basing House was of greater value than any single garrison could be imagined in money, plate, jewels, household stuff and riches. One bed alone was valued at £1,400."[128] The Marquess's cabinet and jewels themselves were worth £50,000. I understand that the value of the pound in those days was the equivalent of £8.10.0. nowadays so that when Oliver Cromwell reported to the House of Commons, "our soldiers have had a good encouragement", he was understating the case. The garrison lost Captain Wiborn, Majors Robinson and Caffaud, and 74 men. But, says Peters, "there may be many more covered with rubbish" (i.e. debris). Six Roman Catholic priests were immediately put to the sword. Such was the intaking of Basing House, which had occupied just two hours according to Hammond. The feeling of savage

---

[126] Mercurius Veridicus No. 25 Complete list in Appendix

[127] Cromwells Report in full in Appendix

[128] Peters Report in full in Appendix

exultancy at this long awaited success is obvious in this contemporary comment; "The enemy tor ought I can learn desired no quarter and had as little offered them; our muskets and swords did show but little compassion and this House being at length subdued did now satisfy for her treason and rebellion by the blood of her defenders."[129]

---

[129] True Informer No. 26

Chapter Eight

'AFTERMATH'

And as the smoke and sparks upward aspire
They'll sit and laugh like Nero at the fire.
                                                    Wm. Webb, 1643.

THROUGHOUT THE DISTRICT the news spread like wildfire, "Basing has fallen, Basing has fallen". In Basingstoke, Bramley, Sherfield, Reading, Alton and a score of other places the farmer left his plough, the innkeeper his tavern, the merchant his shop, the good wife her cooking stove, and counted out their spare cash, then, harnessing their horses to their carts (the bigger the better), they set off post haste to Basing for they knew there would be plunder for sale, everything of the best, at a fraction of its true value. Soon the narrow debris strewn streets of the village were blocked by traffic, everywhere there were groups haggling with the soldiers over rich hangings, costly furniture, and even, perhaps, fine weapons. Food was plentiful. The store houses had yielded 400 quarters of wheat, one hundred bags of malt, hundreds of flitches of bacon, cheese, oatmeal, beef, pork in superabundance.[130] Cellars were crammed with hogsheads of beer and wine. All these were for the taking at bargain prices. Caravans of carts were arriving empty and going away laden high with the Marquess's effects. When the news reached London, the merchants there even hired a hundred horses

---

[130] Peters

and hastened to the scene before it was too late.

Eventually a stop was put to all this bargaining and haggling over stolen goods. A cry even more feared that the plague arose; it was "Fire, fire". During the last siege Dalbier had caused red hot shot to be fired against the House, a primitive form of incendiary weapon. Most of these had been doused with water by the garrison, but one, it is supposed, lay smouldering unperceived. Suddenly a gush of flames swept skyward. One imagines that in the initial stages it could have been extinguished even with the primitive equipment then available. But the crowd stood back and let it burn. Though reprehensible from a historical and moral standpoint, their attitude was understandable. This was the place from which the hated Catholics had defied them for more than two years. Had it not caused the death of two thousand of their comrades, and cost thousands of pounds of the public money to subdue? Let it burn! Perhaps that would teach other Papists and Royalists what happened to those who defied Parliament. And so they stood at a safe distance and let it happen. The like had never been seen before and even they must have been awestruck as the huge bulk of the New House became wrapped in flame throughout its height. The lead melted and sprayed in a molten shower through the gargoyles that normally funneled rain water away. The delicate windows each with its tracery of "Aimez Loyaute" cracked and shattered in the blaze. The great oak beams charred by the furnace-like heat, crackled and then burst into flame until they were so weakened that they gave way, dropping whole floors with their priceless moulded plaster ceilings into the holocaust.

It was now that the prisoners who had been shut up in the vaults and others who had taken refuge in secret hiding places began to scream for help as the heat and smoke penetrated to them.[131] In the general scramble for safety none had thought to release the prisoners. Now it was too late. One wonders how many of the Parliament soldiers were haunted thereafter by the memory of those terrible screams that gradually quavered away into the silence of the tomb? Those poor souls lie there yet for no one has opened the vaults since. The House burned for twenty hours, after which time "there was nothing left but bare walls and chimneys".[132]

Colonel Hammond was sent to the House of Commons to report the intaking of Basing, together with Hugh Peters, who presented to the Speaker the Marquess's own colours, which also bore as a motto "Donec Pax Redeat Terris" (Until peace return to the earth) for which he received a pension of £200 a year. Colonel Hammond who, it will be remembered, was a captive in the House at its taking, was more in a position to describe what ocurred than Cromwell himself in most respects, so on Wednesday, 15 October, it was recorded that "he came this day unto the House of Commons and made a full relation of the taking of Basing House."[133]

The Marquess and Sir Robert Peake had been taken to Basingstoke soon after the fall of the House, where they were lodged in the "Bell" Inn opposite Cromwell's lodging. This place still exists and was until recently occupied by Boots the chemist. Although I have not seen it, I am reliably informed that the room still exists in the basement where malefactors were kept. A local legend states that Cromwell later visited the Marquess to try to persuade him from his allegiance

---

[131] Ibid

[132] Ibid

[133] House of Commons Journal

to the King, but got only irritated replies in return. The Commons ordered that the prisoners should be sent to London with 60 others. On 20 October the Marquess was brought to the bar as a delinquent and the Speaker, William Lenthall, told him: "That for his offence in deserting Parliament and for taking up arms against the Parliament and kingdom contrary to his duty, this House doth for the present commit his Lordship to the Tower, there to be kept in safe custody during the pleasure of the House".[134] Peake and the others were dispersed to various gaols while others more fortunate found their way overseas. Cromwell seems to have been determined to make such an example of Basing House that the garrisons of other places which still held out should be so appalled that they would be much more inclined to surrender on easy terms, for he wrote to the Commons saying: "I humbly offer unto you (Mr. Speaker) to have this place utterly slighted (i.e. demolished) for these following reasons: it will ask about 800 men to manage it, it is no frontier, the country is poor about it, the place exceedingly ruined by our batteries and mortar pieces and by a fire which fell on it since our taking it."[135]

On 15 October in the Journal of the House of Commons there is the following entry: "Resolved, that the house, garrison and walls at Basing be forthwith totally slighted and demolished. Resolved that whosoever will fetch away any stone brick or other materials of Basing House shall have the same for his or their pains".[136] With a large proportion of the cottages in Basing burned by one side or the other during the siege, it seems only just that the villagers, who were

---

[134] House of Commons Journal

[135] Cromwells Report

[136] House of Commons Journal P.309 vol. 4

helpless bystanders in this fight, should be suitably recompensed, and many of the old cottages in Basing can be proved to be built from the materials from the House. Recently in a 17th-century house in Crown Lane I was shown where, during renovations, an bread oven had been uncovered: inset round its mouth were strips of carved marble. There was no doubt whatsoever of its source. And so even the very bones of the great House were carted away to leave only the name of a man who Loved Loyalty to ring down the three hundred years which separate his times from ours.

On 16 October, with many a flourish of trumpet and roll of drums, with flaunting of colours and glint of steel, the long lines of the Parliament Army left a ruined Basing. I feel that the villagers watched them go in silence, not a silence of animosity, but a silence bred of a weariness of spirit. The army passed in order before their eyes. The grim faced Cromwell already preoccupied with the problems of future action flanked by his aides and a cluster of banners followed by the armoured Ironside cavalry, then the heavy cannon which had caused such havoc pulled by straining carthorses, and the musketeers and pikemen carrying their heavy burden with a jaunty step for was there not silver a plenty in their purses? In the rear of the long procession came the baggage train with its attendant escort. Then there was only the sound of the marching feet and the tap of the drum receding into the distance. It was over, finished, done, leaving for posterity only the name and fame of a man who loved loyalty and placed it above all else.

In loving memory of Wilfrid Emberton. Through your words, your memory shall live on, now, always.

BIBLIOGRAPHY

(Those without a date are of recent publication)

Queen Elizabeth's Progresses — J. Nicholls

The History Civil & Ecclesiastical ... of Winchester 2 Vols. — Rev. John Milner 1798-1801

Collections for the History of Hampshire — Richard Warner 1795

General History of Hampshire — Rev. Theodore C. Wilks 1862

Sketches of Hampshire — John Duthy 1839

Hampshire — Robert Mudie 1838

A History of the English Speaking Peoples Vol. 2 — W.S. Churchill

From Hastings to Culloden — Peter Young and John Adair

The Civil War in Hampshire — G.N. Godwin 1882

Antiquities in Hampshire — G. Prosser 1840

Roundhead General — John Adair

The History of the Rebellion — Clarendon 1702

History of Alton — Wm. Curtis 1896

Edgehill, Cropredy Bridge, Marston Moor — all by Peter Young

Victoria County History Vol. 4 (Hampshire)

The Kings War — C. V. Wedgewood

Guns — F. Wilkinson

The Regimental History of Cromwells Army — Sir Charles Firth and Godfrey Davis

Castles and Cannon — B. H. St. J. O'Neil

The full and last relation of all things concerning Basing House, with divers other passages — Hugh Peters report to the House of Commons 1645

A true relation of the marching of the Red Trained Bands of Westminster, The Green Auxiliaries of London and the Yellow Auxiliaries of the Tower Hamlets — Lieutenant Elias Archer 1643

A description of the Siege of Basing Castle kept by the Lord Marquess of Winchester for the Service of his Majesty — Marquess of Winchester's Siege Diary 1644

The Soldiers Report concerning Sir William Waller's fight against Basing House - Anon. 1643

The Gunners Glasse: Wherein the diligent practitioner may see his defects — William Eldred 1646

The Life of the Most Honourable Knight ... Sir Henry Gage 1645

The Great Victory ... obtained by the Forces of Parliament under Sir William Waller at Alton Dec. 1643

The Following Contemporary Newssheets

Mercurius Aulicus — the Cavalier weekly newssheet first appeared in January 1643 priced one penny, published in Oxford

Mercurius Britannicus — the most caustic and continuous of the Parliament newsheets. Sneering and deriding these two publications fought it out on the paper front with malicious zest.

The Scottish Dove — a newsheet issued in London by the Scots gave the news from the Covenanters point of view. At the head of the sheet was the figure of a dove emerging from the Ark and bidding its readers to be "wise as serpents, innocent as doves".

Mercurius Civicus subtitled

London's Intelligencer or Truth impartially related to the whole Kingdom

Mercurius Veridicus or True Information of special and remarkable passages from both Houses of Parliament.

The Moderate Intelligencer — impartially conveying martial affairs to the Kingdom of England.

The Parliament Scout

The Kingdom's Weekly Post

The Weekly Account

The Exact Journal

Other Sources

The Journals of the House of Commons

The Parliamentary Chronicles Three Volumes — John Vicars 1643-46

Woods Life & Times Volume one (1623-1663) collected Andrew Clark 1891

The Army Lists of the Roundheads & Cavaliers containing the names of the officers 1642 edited Edward Peacock 1874.

A great victory obtained by Colonel Norton against Colonel Rayden … neer Walnborough Mill. Published in London 1644

A great overthrow given to Sir Ralph Hopton's Army by Sir Wm Waller's neere Farnham 28 November 1643.

History and Antiquities of Winchester 1773, anonymous but thought to be the work of Rev. Mr. Wavell then master of the hospital of St. Mary Magdalene

APPENDIX 1
THE TREASURE LEGEND

Legend, unsupported by fact, properly has no place in a factual history, yet the legend of the Basing House treasure hoard is so strong, persistent, and ancient that it deserves to be mentioned and a tentative conclusion reached. The legend in its generally accepted form is briefly this: The Marquess of Winchester towards the end of the siege realized that in the end his defeat was inevitable. He wished to save the vast bulk of his fortune, so he melted down his plate into a handily portable form, namely in the shape of animals — generally said to be a calf or calves. These golden treasures were hidden in the House or grounds so cunningly they were never found or reclaimed. Let us take the legend step by step and see what with logic we can accept.

1. It seems reasonable that the Marquess would not wish to allow bis. treasure as well as his House to be taken by Parliament.

2. It is reasonable to suppose that an astute man would leave a proportion of his wealth to be plundered, in sufficient profusion that the Roundheads might suppose they had it all.

3. It is a reasonable conjecture that, with the comparatively low temperature required to melt gold, particularly fine gold, a blacksmith's forge could have been used for this. It is said in the legend that a number of bronze stags had been cast for the ornamentation of the Park in happier times, if the casts had been stored they could have made a handy shape for the casting, and then

with perhaps the servants' help, they could have been sealed away in some secret place.

So far the legend places little strain on our credulity. It could have happened that way. But now comes the difficulties. We must now pose questions which seem to be unanswerable and to if not dispose of the legend in this form, at least to make it dubious .

1. Why was the Marquess allowed to retire to the Continent when he had caused Parliament so much trouble? Could he have bought his life with the treasure secret?

2. Granted that the first possibility is unlikely from a man of the Marquess's dogged tenacity, why did he not reclaim the treasure after the Restoration?

3. If there had been a treasure, would he have been content to live in reduced state in a house that he had inherited from his wife?

But it is possible to look at the legend from another angle. Even for a devout Catholic the Marquess seems to have had a lot of priests in the garrison; some authorities place the number as high as seven. Most of them it seems were of the Jesuit Order. Could it be the fact that these priests brought the treasures from all the Catholic houses in the area or even in the South? Could it be that to save these precious things from profane hands they buried them somewhere in the House and that the secret died with them when they were slaughtered at the intaking of the House? There seems no practical difficulties in our way if we choose to believe in this treasure. It may even be the truth of the matter.

APPENDIX 2
THE TRAINED BANDS

Then as now the defence of the realm depended on the obligation of every able bodied man to rally to the colours when called upon to do so. The old medieval system whereby a land owner was bound to supply a certain number of armed men still appertained. Elizabeth 1st had commanded that each county should also select and train a certain number of its citizens, "to be trained and[137] exercised in such sort as may be reasonably borne by a common charge of the whole county".

In the time of Charles I the trained bands as these regiments were called were a laughing stock. They were supposed to meet to train once a month but few took it seriously. All of the practising military men who wrote the drill books of the time were troubled about this. Colonel Robert Ward commented that "by the time the arms be all viewed and the muster master has his pay it draws toward dinner time, and indeed officers love their bellies so well that they are loth to take too much pains on the discipling of their soldiers .... Wherefore after a little careless hurrying over their

postures (drill) with which they are little bettered ... every man repairs home ...".[138]

The God they worship is not Mars but Bacchus, commented Captain Thomas Venn bitterly.[139] William Barriffe (a Lieutenant at

---

[137] Gross: Military Antiquities 1, 87

[138] Ward: Animadversions of War 1639

[139] Venn: Military Discipline 1672

the time of writing his book) stated plainly "No man is born a soldier, nor can attain to any excellency in that art except through practice .... though small hope of amendment (of this state of unreadiness) seeing that our soldiers are scarce called forth to excercise either postures or motions once or twice in four or five years".[140]

The only place where the trained bands reached any stage of proficience was in London where small military societies met at the Artillery Garden in Bishopsgate and the Military Garden in St. Martins fields to learn the trade under the tuition of hired professionals.

Venn dedicated his book to one such society "to the most truly generous gentlemen and cityzens of London practicing arms in the Artillery Garden".

Thanks to these forward looking gentlemen who officered the regiments the London trained bands were the only militia who made a significant contribution to the Parliamentary war effort. At their general muster in Finsbury Fields on 28 September 1643 they were eight regiments consisting of 10,894 officers and men.[141]

---

[140] Bariffe: The Young Artilleryman 1639

[141] Lord Dillon's M.S.

APPENDIX 3
ORGANISATION AT FINAL STORM AT BASING

Captain: Marquess Winchester Col.

Captain: Sir Robert Peake Lt. Col.; Lieutenant: Patrick Quayle; Ensign: Wm. Faithorne

Captain: John Caffaud Major

Captain: Peregrine Tasborough

Captain: William Payne

Captain: John Snow; Lieutenant: Francis Massey

Captain: Tatteshall; Ensign: Thos. Tonstall

Captain: —. Wyburn; Lieutenant: Possibly Reformadoes (officers whose regiments have been disbanded)

Captain: Tamworth Reresby

Captain: —. Rigby

APPENDIX 4
NAMES OF WINCHESTER'S OFFICERS
A LIST OF [INDIGENT] OFFICERS (1663)

John Paulet, Marquis of Winchester

L&W.[142] Francis Cuffaud, Capt. — Lieutenant (Horse)

Hampshire. Hugh Clancy, Lieutenant

L&W. Peregrine Tasborough, Captain (Foot)

L&W. Wiliam Payne, Captain

Hertfordshire. John Snow, Captain

L&W. Francis Massey, Lieutenant

L&W. Patrick Quoyle, Lieutenant

L&W. Will Faithorne, Ensign to Lieut. Col. Peake

Hampshire. John Cleere, Lieutenant

L&W. Rand Hankinson Ensign

Lincoln. Thomas Tonstall, Ensign to Capt. Tatteshall

Hampshire. Bold Wakefield, Ensign

---

[142] He was a Hampshire man, but he was probably in London, hanging about the Court and hoping for some employment.

APPENDIX 5
LIST OF THE GARRISON OF BASING HOUSE
NOVEMBER 1644

GOVERNOR: John Paulet Marquis of Winchester. Colonel
LT. GOVERNOR: Sir Robert Peake. Lt. Colonel
MAJOR: John Cuffaud
1st CAPTAIN: Peregrine Tasbury
2nd CAPTAIN: William Payne.
Total: 200 foot.

MILITARY GOVERNOR: Sir Marmaduke Rawdon. Colonel
1st LT. COLONEL: Thomas Johnson
2nd LT. COLONEL: Thomas Langley
MAJOR: William Rowsewell
1st CAPTAIN: Isaac Rowlett
2nd CAPTAIN: Robert Emery [or Amery]
5 Companies: 200 foot.

Horse. 1st troop (Marquess of Winchester's) Lieutenant Francis Cuffaud
2nd troop Lieut. Colonel Sir Robert Peake
Total: 100 horse

Thus the garrison at this time totals 500.[143]

---

[143] Richard Symonds. BM Harlisan MSS 986

APPENDIX 6
AFTER THE TAKING OF BASING HOUSE, OCTOBER 15TH, 1645

KILLED

Major Castle

Major Cuffaud

Major Robinson

Captain Wiborn

Captain Rigby

Messrs. Salvine, Bowler — volunteers.

PRISONERS OF WAR

Colonel John Paulet, Marquess of Winchester

Lt. Colonel Sir Robert Peake

Captain-Lieutenant Francis Cuffaud (Horse)

Captain Tattershall (Foot)

Captain Peregrine Tasborough

Captain Tamworth Reresby

Captain John Snow

Captain William Payne

Lieutenant Hugh Glausie (Irish) [Clancy]

Lieutenant Francis Massey

Lieutenant William Faithorne

Lieutenant —, Rowlett

Lieutenant —, Beck

Cornet Francis Hide

Ensign Thomas Tunstall (Tattershalls Coy.)

Sergeant Henry Payne

Sergeant Christopher Kenton

Sergeant John Light

Sergeant Richard Foxall

Quartermaster John Foy

Corporal William Hare

Corporal James Ellis

Thomas Webb, Clerk

William Morgan and Edward Cole (Catholic Priests)

Humphrey Vanderblin (probably an engineer)

William Smithson (his servant)

Ensigns of Foot: Thomas Antell, Roger Coram, John Weston, Oliver Lloyd

APPENDIX 7
OFFICERS FOR SIR MARMADUKE RAWDON'S REGIMENT
A LIST OF [INDIGENT] OFFICERS (1663)

L&W. Rob Emery, Captain

Cambridge. Will Pildrim. Lieut.

Captain —, Fletcher

Somerset. John Brown Lieutenant

L&W. Giles Teadman, Ensign to Capt. Isaac Rowlett

L&W. William Murray Ensign

L&W. John Fauntleroy Ensign

APPENDIX 8
LIEUTENANT GENERAL OLIVER CROMWELL'S ARMY AT BASING

COLONEL THOMAS SHEFFIELD'S REGIMENT (HORSE)

The Colonel's Troop: 11 officers and 84 troopers

Captain Sheffield's Troop: 10 officers and 70 troopers

Captain Hagle's Troop: 10 officers and 70 troopers

Captain Flynne's Troop: 11 officers and 71 troopers

Captain Robotham's Troop: 90 officers and 63 troopers

Captain Wogone's Troop: 10 officers and 53 troopers

Total: 61 officers and 414 troopers

Standard: An armed horseman with the motto *Deo duce, nil desperandum*.

COLONEL MONTAGU'S REGIMENT

Dress: Colour of Coats: Blue

Lieut. Colonel Grimes

Major Kelsey

Captains Blethen, Munney, Biscoe, Rogers, Wilks, Thomas, Disney and Sanders

LIEUTENANT GENERAL OLIVER CROMWELL; (HORSE)

Dress: Steel Plates front and back: Steel headpieces

Major Huntingdon

1st Captain —. Jenkins

2nd Captain —. Middleton

3rd Captain John Reynolds

4th Captain —. Blackwell

In each troop 100 strong.

COLONEL SIR HARDRESS WALLER'S REGIMENT

Dress: Colour of Coats: Black

Lieut. Colonel Cottesworth

Major —. Smith

1st Captain Howard

2nd Captain Wade

3rd Captain Ashe

4th Captain Gorges

5th Captain Clark

6th Captain Thomas

7th Captain Hodden

COLONEL ROBERT HAMMOND'S REGIMENT (HORSE)

Lieut. Colonel Thomas Eure

Major Sanders

Captain Disney

Captain Charn

Captain Smith

Captain John Boyce

Captain Puckle

Captain Stratton

Captain Rolfe

COLONEL CHARLES FLEETWOOD'S REGIMENT (HORSE)

Major Harrison

Captain Coleman
Captain Laughton
Captain Zanchy
Captain Howard

Possibly not all these officers were present at Basing, as the lists from which this has been compiled were made before or after the intaking.

APPENDIX 9
PRICES OF ARMOUR

By an order made in 1629 the following prices fixed for armour. This is a good guide also to what the various types of soldier wore. The suggestion that the 17th century pound would buy £8.10.0. worth of goods today has been obtained from a reliable source.

CUIRRASIER:

A breast of pistol proofe: 11/-

A backe: 7/-

A close caske (helmet) lined: 17/-

A payre of pouldrons: 12/-

A payre of vambraces: 12/-

A payre of guissets: 17/-

A cullet or garderine: 7/-

A gorget lined: 3/6

A gauntlet gloved: 3/6

So the whole price of the cuirrasiers armour amounted to £3.10.0.

The price of the parts and of the whole corselet or footman's armour russeted viz:

The breast: 5/6

The back: 4/6

The tassets: 5/-

The combined headpiece (lyned): 4/6

The gorget (lined): 4/6

The total of the footmans armour — £1.2.6.

If the breast back and tassets be lined with red leather the price will be £1.4.6.

The prices of the parts and of the whole armour for a harquebusier on horseback russeted viz:
A breast of pistoll proofe: 9/-
A back: 7/-
A gorgett: 3/-
A headpiece with great cheeks and bar before the face: 11/-
A combed headpiece for a musketter russet ted and lined: 5/-

Price of the pike:
The staffe: 2/6
The head: 1/8
Socket and colouring: 4d.
Summe: 4/6
For a new musket with worm mould and scourer: 15/6

For a new bandolier with twelve charges, a prymer, a pryming wyre, a bullet back, a strap or belt 2 inches in breadth: 2/6.

For a pair of horseman's pistols, furnished with snaphances, mouldes, wormes scourer and charger and cases: £2.

APPENDIX 10
WILLIAM ELDRED IN THE GUNNERS GLASSE 1646
CANNON IN USE IN THE CIVIL WAR

Cannon Royal
Calibre in inches: 8
Weight of piece in lbs.: 8,000
Length of piece in ft.: 8
Weight of shot in lbs.: 63

Cannon
Calibre in inches: 7
Weight of piece in lbs.: 7,000
Length of piece in ft.: 10
Weight of shot in lbs.: 47

Demi Cannon
Calibre in inches: 6
Weight of piece in lbs.: 6,000
Length of piece in ft.: 12
Weight of shot in lbs.: 27

Culverin
Calibre in inches: 5
Weight of piece in lbs.: 4,000
Length of piece in ft.: 11
Weight of shot in lbs.: 15

Demi Culverin

Calibre in inches: 4½

Weight of piece in lbs.: 3,600

Length of piece in ft.: 10

Weight of shot in lbs.: 9

Saker

Calibre in inches: 3½

Weight of piece in lbs.: 2,500

Length of piece in ft.: 9½

Weight of shot in lbs.: 5¼

Minion

Calibre in inches: 3

Weight of piece in lbs.: 1,500

Length of piece in ft.: 8

Weight of shot in lbs.: 4

Falcon

Calibre in inches: 2¾

Weight of piece in lbs.: 700

Length of piece in ft.: 6

Weight of shot in lbs.: 2¼

Falconet

Calibre in inches: 2

Weight of piece in lbs.: 210

Length of piece in ft.: 4

Weight of shot in lbs.: 1¼

Robinet

Calibre in inches: 1¼

Weight of piece in lbs.: 120

Length of piece in ft.: 3

Weight of shot in lbs.: ¾

Eldred who describes himself as "sometime master gunner of Dover Castle" published his book in 1646. It contains 107 pages and is a mine of information for those interested in the artillery of the period and sets out in the form of a dialogue between "gunner" and "scholar" all the intricacies of the art of gunnery with very many explanations of a practical nature. It must have been indispensable for the fledgling gunner of the time and an efficient aide memoire for the expert.

APPENDIX 11

COMPARATIVE RATES OF PAY IN 1644

Royalist

Captain: £2.12. 6.

Lieutenant: 1. 8.0.

Ensign: 1. 1.0.

Sergeant: 10. 6.

Corporal: 7.0.

Drummer: 7. 0.

Soldier: 4.0.

Weekly

Parliament

Colonel: £63. 0.0.

Lieut. Colonel: 42. 0.0.

Major: 33. 0.0.

Captain: 7. 0.0.

Lieutenant: 5. 12. 0.

Ensign: 4. 4.0.

Sergeant: 2. 2.0.

Corporal: 1. 17.4.

Drummer: 1. 7.0.

Monthly

There were no standard rates of pay, these are examples given by Brigadier Young's book "Edgehill", quoting Richard Symonds diary for the Royalists and an order from the Earl of Essex to the

Earl of Stamford for the other. Troops of both sides were frequently in arrears of pay, and the letters from commanders of both sides are full of warning that their troops will disband unless the discrepancy was made good.

APPENDIX 12
THE SPOILS

The most complete list of the spoil comes from Mercurius Veridicus the Parliament Newsheet No. 25 as follows:—

List of what was taken at Basing by Lieutenant General Cromwell and Colonel Dalbier on Tuesday, October, 14th 1645

10 pieces of Ordnance

20 barrels of Gunpowder

9 Colours

2000 arms

200 horses

300 slain and burned

180 taken prisoner

20 Gentlewomen taken

1 Gallant gentlewoman slain

6 priests slain

4 priests taken prisoner

£8000 worth of beads, clothes and other goods

Many firkins of butter

Much bullet and match

All their ammunition taken

Bag and Baggage

Many books of them divers Popish

A great many crucifixes and Popish pictures taken

1000 chests, trunks and boxes

400 qtrs. of corn

200 barrels of beef

300 flitches of bacon

4000 lbs weight of cheese

The Marquess' plate worth £5000

The Marquess' cabinet and jewels

Sir Robert Peake's plate worth £500

The Marquess' own bed and furniture cost £1300

£300 gold taken in one hole by one soldier

One cabinet of jewels burned

Sir Robert Peake's box of jewels, rings and bracelets

A box of brass graven plates of Sir Robert Peakes

100 gentlewomans rich gowns and petticoats

A great quantity of wine

Many hogsheads of beer

The Marquess taken, Sir Robert Peake and (Sir) Inigo Jones taken, Robinson the fool slain as he was acting and turning like a player, Doctor Griffiths sometime minister of Dunstans London fore wounded and taken prisoner with his daughters.

The Marquess and some with him had quarter by Articles for releasing C. Ham and M. King

APPENDIX 13
CONTEMPORARY DOCUMENTS
REFERRING TO THE SIEGE

Although I have adopted the modern spelling for the convenience of the reader, I have preserved the original sense of these reports.

Lieutenant General Cromwell's letter sent to the Honourable William Lenthall, Speaker of the Honourable House of Commons, concerning the storming and taking of Basing House with the Marquess of Winchester, Sir Robert Peake and divers other Officers of Quality and all the Ordnance Ammunition, Arms and provisions therein.

SIR, I thank God I can give you a good account of Basing. After our batteries were placed we set the various posts for the storm. Colonel Dalbier was to be on the North side of the House next the Grange, Colonel Pickering on his left hand and Sir Hardress Waller and Colonel Montagues next him. We stormed this morning after six of the clock the signal for falling on was the firing of four of our cannon which being done our men fell on with great resolution and cheerfulness. We took the two houses without any considerable loss to ourselves. Colonel Pickering stormed the New House passed through and got the Gate of the Old House whereupon they summoned a parley which our men would not hear. In the meantime Colonel Montague and Sir Hardress Wallers' regiments assaulted the strongest work where the enemy kept his court of

Guard which with great resolution they recovered beating the enemy from a whole Culverin and from that work, which having done they drew their ladders up after them, and got over another work and the house wall before they could enter. In this Sir Hardress Waller performing his duty with honour and diligence was shot on this arm but not dangerous. We have little loss, many of the enemy our men put to the swprd and some officers of quality, most of the rest we have prisoners, amongst which the Marquess and Sir Robert Peake, with divers other officers whom I have ordered to be sent up to you. We have taken about ten pieces of Ordnance much ammunition and our soldiers a good encouragement. I humbly offer to you, to have this place slighted (i.e. demolished) for these reasons. It will ask (i.e. require) eight hundred men to man it. It is no frontier, the country is poor about it, the place exceedingly ruined by our batteries and mortar pieces and a fire which fell upon the place since our taking it. If you please to take the garrison at Farnham some out of Chichester and a good part of the foot that were here under Dalbier and make a strong quarter at Newbury with three or four troops of horse, I dare be confident it would not only be a curb to Donnington but a security and a frontier to all these parts in as much as Newbury lies on the river and will prevent an incursion from Donnington, Wallingford or Faringdon into these parts and by lying there will make the trade most secure between Bristol and London for all carriages. And I believe the gentlemen of Sussex and Hampshire will with more cheerfulness contribute to maintain a garrison on the Frontier, than in the bowels which will have less safety in it.

Sir, I hope not to delay but march toward the West tomorrow and be as diligent as I may in my expedition thither, I must speak my judgement to you that if you intend to have your work carried out, Recruits of foot must be had and course taken to pay your army else, believe me sir, it may not be able to answer all the work you have for it to do. I entreated Colonel Hammond to wait upon you who was taken by a mistake while we lay before this garrison, whom God lately delivered to us to our great joy, but to his loss of almost everything he had, which the enemy took from him. The Lord grant that these mercies may be acknowledged with all thankfulness, God exceedingly abounds in his goodness to us and will not be weary until Righteousness and peace meet and that he hath brought forth a glorious work for the happiness of this poor kingdom and wherein desires to serve God and you with a faithfull hand.

Your most humble servant,

Oliver Cromwell

Basingstoke

14th October 1645.

A DAY OF THANKSGIVING PROCLAIMED BY PARLIAMENT 15TH OCTOBER 1645

Ordered by the Commons in Parliament assembled that the next Lords Day public thanks be given unto Almighty God for his great mercies and blessings upon the Parliaments forces under Lieutenant General Cromwell and Colonel Dalbier (for taking in Winchester Castle and Basing House) in all Churches and Chaples in the cities of London and Westminster and within the lines of communications. And Alderman Pennington and Colonel Venn are appointed by this house to desire the Lord Mayor to give timely notice hereof to the Minister of the Churches and Chapels within the lines of communication.

The full and last relation of all things concerning Basing House with divers other passages, represented to Mr. Speaker and divers members in the House. By Mr. Peters who came from Lieutenant General Cromwell, also how there are strange and hideous cries heard in the ground. Commanded to be Printed and Published according to Order. London Printed by Jane Coe 1645.

On Wednesday, the 15th of October 1645, Mr. Peters came from Basing upon some special concernments of the Army and upon Thursday morning early was in the House with the Speaker and divers members and according to their desire gave full account of some things concerning Basing not in the Lieutenant General's letter which was to this purpose. That Mr. Peters came into the House of Basing some time after the storm on Tuesday, the 14th

October, 1645, (misprinted in the original 1465) and took a view, first of the works which were many but not finished, and of too great a compass, for so few men to keep Sir Robert Peake the Governor swearing to him that they had but 300 fighting men in all, the circumference being about a mile and a half about, there were in both houses 16 Courtyards great and small, the old house has stood as it is reported 2 or 300 years, a nest of idolatry, the new house surpassing that in beauty and stateliness and either of them fit to make an Emperors court. The rooms before the storm (it seems) in both houses were all completely furnished, provisions for some years rather than months. 400 quarters of wheat, bacons, divers rooms full, hundreds of flitches of bacon, cheese proportional with oatmeal, beef, pork, beer divers cellars full, and that very good. A bed in one room furnished that cost £1,300 Popish books very many, with Copes and such utensils that in truth the house stood in its full pride and the enemy was persuaded that it would be the last piece of ground that would be taken by Parliament because they had so often failed our forces, that had formerly appeared before it. In the several rooms and about the house, there were slain in view and only one woman, the daughter of Dr. Griffiths who came forth railing against our soldiers for their rough handling (ruffecarriages) toward her father, who indeed did remember to him his former malignancy there lay on the ground slain by the hand of Major Harrison (that godly and gallant gentleman). Major Cuffle a man of great account amongst them and a notorious Papist and Robinson the player, who a little before the storm was known to be mocking and scorning the Parliament and our army. Eight or nine gentlewomen of rank running forth together were entertained by the common soldiers somewhat coarsely, yet not uncivilly, they left them with some clothes on them. Their plunder continued until Tuesday night in this manner. For the goods the soldiers seized on the first goods of which there were several sorts, one soldier had six score pieces in gold for his share, others plate, others jewels amongst the rest one got three bags of silver who (not being able to keep his own counsel) it grew to be common pillage amongst the rest, the fellow himself had but one half crown left for himself at last.

There were four rich cabinets of jewels and other rich treasure next to that, the soldiers sold the wheat to the country people and the price held a while to the country people but afterward the market fell and there was some abatements by half. After that they sold the household stuff whereof there was good store and they loaded away many carts and continued a great while fetching out all manner of household stuff till they had fetched out the stools chairs and other lumber all of which, they sold to the country people, by pricemeal which was admirable, that in all these great houses there was not one iron bar left in all the windows, save only what was in the fire by night. The last of all was the lead and by Thursday morning there was hardly any left of that.

2. For the fire, what the soldiers left the fire took hold on, joy was more then ordinary leaving nothing but bare walls and chimneys in less than twenty hours, and occasioned by the neglect of the enemy in quenching a fireball of ours.

We know not how to give an just account of all that was within, for we have not 200 prisoners and it may be 100 slain, whose bodies some being covered by rubbish, come not into view, only riding to the house on Tuesday night, we heard divers crying in vaults for quarter but our men could neither come to them nor they to us. But amongst those we saw slain one of their officers seeming so exceeding tall was measured and from the crown of his head to his great toe was 9 foot in length being measured by an gentleman of an ordinary size who was then present. There was in all (in the House) about 500 besides some that before got out of the house. And it is reported there are some vaults that are far underground for their popish priests of which cattle there were various, but none came into our hands how many of them we killed we know not.

3. Mr. Peters spent some time in conference with the Marquess of Winchester and Sir Robert Peake the Governor one of Mr. Peters neighbours when he lived in the parish of sepulchres. The Marquess, pressed by him by way of argument broke out and said, if the King had no more ground in England but Basing House, he would adventure himself as he did and so maintain it to the uttermost (meaning with those Papists) and the Marquess said .himself that Basing House was called Loyalty. But he was soon silenced in the matter of King and Parliament, only hoping the King might have a day again.

4. We see who are his Majesty's dear friends and trusty and well beloved counselors, the Marquess being the Popes devoted vasall.

5. And thus the Lord was pleased in a few hours to show us what mortal seed all earthly glory grows upon and how just and righteous the ways of God are who takes sinners in their own snares and lifteth up the head of his despised people.

Printed in Great Britain
by Amazon